THE OFFICIAL MTO MOTORCYCLE HANDBOOK

This handbook is only a guide. For official purposes, please refer to the *Ontario Highway Traffic Act* and regulations.

For more information about driver licensing, visit www.mto.gov.on.ca.

To request a copy of this book in an alternate format, contact Publications Ontario at 1-800-668-9938 or (416) 326-5300 or visit www.publications.serviceontario.ca.

Disponible en français
Demandez le « Guide officiel des motocyclettes publié par le MTO »

DRIVING IS A PRIVILEGE — NOT A RIGHT.

INTRODUCTION

This handbook provides guidelines for drivers of motorcycles, three-wheeled motorcycles, limited-speed motorcycles (LSMs) and motor-assisted bicycles (mopeds). Unless stated otherwise, references to motorcycles in this handbook include three-wheeled motorcycles and limited-speed motorcycles.

Motorcycle and moped driving can be an enjoyable, even exciting, experience — but it can also be dangerous. As a driver of one of the smallest vehicles on the road, you are more likely to be injured or killed if you are involved in a collision. To avoid collisions and survive, you must learn to drive carefully and safely.

Driver error is the most common cause of traffic collisions. A large percentage of fatal collisions among motorcycle and moped drivers is due to losing control while speeding.

The Ontario Ministry of Transportation encourages new motorcycle and moped drivers, and those who wish to improve their skills, to take a motorcycle-safety training course. For information about motorcycle-safety training, or a course being conducted near you, call your local community college or check the Ministry of Transportation website at www.mto.gov.on.ca. Remember that this handbook is only a guide.

The *Official MTO Driver's Handbook* provides information that is required for users of all motor vehicles. **The *Official MTO Motorcycle Handbook* must be used in conjunction with the *Official MTO Driver's Handbook*.**

For official descriptions of the laws, check the *Highway Traffic Act of Ontario* and its regulations, as well as the *Motorized Snow Vehicles Act* and the *Off-Road Vehicles Act of Ontario* at www.e-laws.gov.on.ca. Information on how to get licences to drive other types of vehicles is available in the *Official MTO Driver's Handbook*, the *Official MTO Truck Handbook*, the *Official MTO Bus Handbook* and the *Official MTO Air Brake Handbook*. To find out how to get these publications, please see page 120.

CONTENTS

CONTENTS

CHAPTER 1
GETTING YOUR MOTORCYCLE LICENCE

This chapter tells you what licence you need to drive a motorcycle, a motor tricycle, a limited-speed motorcycle (LSM) and a motor-assisted bicycle (moped) in Ontario, whether you are a new driver, a visitor or a new resident. It explains the graduated licensing system, including the tests you will have to pass and the driving privileges you will have at each licence level.

Types of vehicles requiring a class M licence

There are four types of vehicles for which you require a motorcycle class of licence to drive on public roads in Ontario: motorcycles, motor tricycles, limited-speed motorcycles (LSMs) and motor-assisted bicycles (mopeds).

A restricted class M licence for motor tricycles has a condition that will allow licence holders to drive three-wheeled motorcycles only.

I. MOTORCYCLES

The Ontario Highway Traffic Act (HTA) defines a motorcycle as a self-propelled vehicle with a seat or saddle for the driver, designed to travel with not more than three wheels in contact with the ground.

Three-wheeled motorcycles are commonly referred to as motor tricycles. A three-wheeled motorcycle may have either two front wheels or two rear wheels, or may be a two-wheeled motorcycle with a sidecar.

Motor tricycles manufactured to comply with the *HTA*'s motorcycle definition can be registered to drive on Ontario's public roads only if they:

- Have seating on which all occupants must sit astride
- Do not have more than four designated seating positions
- Do not have a gross vehicle weight rating of greater than 1,000 kilograms
- Do not have a structure partially or fully enclosing the driver and passenger, other than that part of the vehicle forward of the driver's torso and the seat backrest

Vehicles commonly referred to as motor scooters are considered motorcycles. Depending on the characteristics of the vehicle, a motor scooter may be considered a limited-speed motorcycle.

Motorcycles must be registered with the Ministry of Transportation and have a valid motorcycle licence plate attached in order to be driven on public roads in Ontario.

Note: In this handbook, unless stated otherwise, the term "motorcycle" includes motor tricycles and limited-speed motorcycles.

II. LIMITED-SPEED MOTORCYCLES (LSMS)

A limited-speed motorcycle is a motorcycle to which the manufacturer has affixed a compliance label, as required by the *Motor Vehicle Safety Act* (Canada), which indicates the vehicle type as "LSM/MVL."

Typically, LSMs are gas powered, cannot go faster than 70 km/h, have a "step-through design" and automatic transmission.

If the vehicle was manufactured before September 1, 1988, and does not have a label, it is a limited-speed motorcycle if it has all of the following characteristics:

- Minimum attainable speed of 32 km/h on level ground within 1.6 kilometres from a standing start
- Maximum speed of 70 km/h or less
- Steering handlebars that are completely restrained from rotating in relation to the axle of only one wheel in contact with the ground
- Minimum seat height, when not laden, of 650 millimetres
- Minimum wheel-rim diameter of 250 millimetres
- Minimum wheelbase of 1,016 millimetres
- Engine displacement of 50 cubic centimetres or less

Limited-speed motorcycles must be registered with the Ministry of Transportation and have a valid limited-speed motorcycle licence plate or a regular motorcycle licence plate attached in order to be driven on public roads.

III. MOTOR-ASSISTED BICYCLES (MOPEDS)

A moped has the following characteristics:
- Weight of 55 kilograms or less
- Attached motor driven by electricity or having a piston displacement of no more than 50 cubic centimetres
- Pedals that are operable at all times and may be used to propel the moped
- No hand- or foot-operated clutch or gearbox driven by the motor and transferring power to the driven wheel
- Maximum speed of 50 km/h on level ground within 2 kilometres from a standing start

Under the *Highway Traffic Act*, mopeds are not considered motorcycles; however, mopeds require you to have the same types of riding skills as required for motorcycles, and you must hold a valid motorcycle class licence (an M1, M2(L), M2, M(L) or M) in order to drive on Ontario's public roads. Your moped must also be registered with the Ministry of Transportation and have a valid moped licence plate attached. When registering your moped at a ServiceOntario centre, you must show the new vehicle information statement (NVIS). If your moped is a 1983 or earlier model, and you do not have an NVIS, you may make a self-declaration that the vehicle is a moped as defined under the *Highway Traffic Act*. After registering, you will be given a vehicle permit and a moped licence plate.

What you need to drive a motorcycle, a motor tricycle, a limited-speed motorcycle and a moped in Ontario

In Ontario, there are 12 different classes of licence. Each class qualifies you to drive a different type of vehicle. The class of licence you have must match the type of vehicle you are driving. You need a Class G licence to drive a car, van or small truck. You must have a Class G licence before you can be licensed to drive most other types of vehicles. The only exception to this rule is motorcycles and mopeds; an applicant for a class M licence may get a Class M licence without first getting a Class G licence. A class G licence holder may not drive a motorcycle without a class M licence.

To drive a motorcycle you must be at least 16 years old and have a valid motorcycle licence (Class M1, M2 or M).

You must have the proper type of licence plate attached to the rear of your motorcycle or moped, as well as valid vehicle registration. You must also have liability insurance. Carry your driver's licence, vehicle registration and insurance card with you in case a police officer asks to see them.

An applicant will have a condition added to their class M licence, if they pass the Level One or Level Two road test in a motorcycle that is not a full class M vehicle.

- The M condition is added to your licence if you pass the Level One or Level Two road test using a three-wheeled motorcycle. The M condition means you are licensed to drive a three-wheeled motorcycle only.
- The L condition is added to your licence if you pass the Level One or Level Two road test using a limited-speed motorcycle or moped. The L condition means you are licensed to drive either a limited-speed motorcycle or a moped only.

Graduated licensing

New drivers applying for their first car or motorcycle licence enter Ontario's graduated licensing system. Graduated licensing lets new drivers gain driving experience and skills gradually. The two-step licensing process takes at least 20 months to complete.

To apply for a motorcycle licence, you must be at least 16 years old. When you apply, you will be asked questions about your health. People with some types of physical or medical conditions are not allowed to drive for safety reasons. If your physical or medical condition means you cannot be licensed, you will be told when you apply.

You must pass a vision test and a written test of your knowledge of traffic signs. You must also pass a written test of your knowledge of motorcycles and the rules of the road. There is a fee charged for these tests.

After you pass these tests, you enter Level One and get a Class M1 licence.

You must pass two road tests to become fully licenced. Passing the Level One road test gives you a Class M2 licence and you move to Level Two. Passing the Level Two road test gives you a full Class M driver's licence.

Road tests

Road tests check your skill at handling a motorcycle or moped and driving one on the road. You will be tested on your ability to apply the rules of the road and safe driving practices.

The Level One road test deals with basic driving skills. The Level Two road test deals with advanced knowledge and skills that are generally gained with driving experience. Your performance in each of these tests will tell you whether you need more training or practice. All road

tests have a set time frame. Before you begin your test, your examiner will tell you how much time you have to complete it.

Motorcycle safety courses:

The Ministry of Transportation encourages all new drivers to take a ministry-approved motorcycle safety course to help learn the proper driving skills and required knowledge. This course can be taken in Level One or Level Two and includes a road test. If you pass a ministry-approved course, you can reduce the time you must spend at Level Two, and you may qualify for a reduction in insurance premiums.

Level One - Class M1

To enter Level One, you must be at least 16 years old. You must pass a vision test and a written test of your knowledge of traffic signs. You must also pass a written test of your knowledge of motorcycles and the rules of the road.

Level One knowledge test - checklist:

Before attempting the knowledge test, be sure to study this handbook, as well as chapter 2, "Safe and responsible driving," and chapter 3, "Traffic signs and lights," in the *Official MTO Driver's Handbook*. Bring the following items to the knowledge test:
- Two pieces of identification (see *MTO Driver's Handbook* for acceptable documents)
- Money for test fees – cash, debit or credit card
- Glasses or contact lenses (if you need to wear them to read or write)

Once you pass the vision and knowledge tests, you get a Class M1 licence and enter Level One. You must stay at Level One for a minimum of 60 days from the day you obtained your M1 licence, after which you may attempt the Level One road test.

The M1 licence is only valid for 90 days, so it is a good idea to book your Level One road test early in order to complete it before your M1 licence expires.

Graduated licensing requirements

Here are the rules you must follow at each level:

While at Level One

With an M1 licence, you may drive a motorcycle, motor tricycle, a limited-speed motorcycle or a moped, under the following conditions:

- You must not drive if you have been drinking alcohol. Your blood-alcohol level must be zero.
- You must drive only during daylight hours — one-half hour before sunrise to one-half hour after sunset.
- You must not drive on roads with speed limits of more than 80 km/h, except highways 11, 17, 61, 69, 71, 101, 102, 144

and 655. (These exceptions are made because some drivers have no other route available to them.)
- You must not carry passengers.

Level One road test

You must pass a road test of your driving skills to obtain a class M2 licence and move to Level Two. When you book the road test, you will be required to indicate the type of vehicle you plan to bring to the test (for example, motorcycle, limited-speed motorcycle or moped). The type of motorcycle you bring to the test will determine the type of licence you will receive.

If you pass the test using a limited-speed motorcycle or moped, you get an M2 licence with an L condition. The L condition restricts you to driving a limited-speed motor-cycle or moped on public roads other than controlled-access highways and any other highways listed in Reg. 630 of the *Highway Traffic Act*.

If you pass the test on a three-wheeled motorcycle (motor tricycle or motorcycle with sidecar), you will receive an M2 licence with an M condition. The M condition will restrict you to driving only three-wheeled motorcycles on any public road in Ontario.

If you pass the test on a motor-cycle other than a three-wheeled motorcycle or a limited-speed motorcycle, you get an M2 licence (no L or M condition), and you may drive a motorcycle or motor tricycle on any public road in Ontario. You may also drive a moped or limited-speed motorcycle on public roads where they are permitted.

Level One road test - checklist

Before taking the Level One road test, make sure you have studied the *Official MTO Driver's Handbook* and the *Official MTO Motorcycle Handbook*.

Bring the following items to the test:
- Vehicle in good working order (see "Out-of-order road test" on page 16 in this handbook)
- M1 driver's licence
- Approved motorcycle helmet (helmets that comply with Regulation 610 of the *Highway Traffic Act*)
- Glasses or contact lenses (if you need to wear them to drive)

Arrive at least 30 minutes before the road test appointment.

Please note: If you take your Level One road test as part of a ministry-approved motorcycle safety course, you must still wait 60 days minimum to move to Level Two. Remember that the course certificate is valid for only six months. Be sure to take it to a DriveTest Centre after the 60 days but before the six months have passed, or you will have to take your road test again.

Level Two - Class M2 or M2(L), or M2(M)

Level Two lasts a minimum of 22 months from the day you obtain your M2 or M2(L), or M2 (M) licence. However, if you pass a ministry-approved motorcycle safety course, you can reduce the time spent at Level Two by four months. You may stay at Level Two for a maximum of five years from the day you pass your Level One road test. You must either attempt the Level Two road test to move to a full-class M, M (M), or M(L) licence or re-apply for Level Two before your Level Two licence expires at the end of the five years.

While at Level Two

At Level Two you have more privileges because of your driving experience.
- You may drive at night.
- You may carry passengers (except on a moped).

- With an M2 licence, you may drive a motorcycle or motor tricycle on any public road. You may also drive a limited-speed motorcycle or a moped on any public road other than those listed in Regulation 630 of the *Highway Traffic Act*.
- If you have an M2(L) licence, you may drive a limited-speed motorcycle or moped on any public road other than those listed in Regulation 630 of the *Highway Traffic Act*.
- If you have a Class M2 (M) licence, you may not drive a two-wheeled motorcycle, limited-speed motorcycle, or moped.
- If you have a valid Class M2, M2(L), or M2(M) licence, you may also drive Class G vehicles under the conditions that apply to a Class G1 licence. Please see the *Official MTO Driver's Handbook* for more information on Class G licences.

Do not:

- Drive your motorcycle or moped if you have been drinking alcohol; your blood-alcohol level must be zero
- Carry passengers on a moped; it is an offence under the *Highway Traffic Act*

Level Two road test

After you have completed the time required at Level Two, you may take the Level Two road test to qualify for full-class M licence privileges.

Before taking the Level Two test on a motorcycle that is not limited-speed, you must complete a declaration of highway driving experience form, on which you will describe your experience driving a motorcycle on highways with speed limits of 80 km/h or greater.

LSMs and mopeds at the M2 level are allowed to drive on all highways except for the controlled-access freeways listed in Regulation 630, so if you take the M2 road test on a limited-speed motorcycle, or moped, you do not complete the freeway driving section of the test. However, you will be required to drive on 50 km/h roads. Before taking the Level Two test on a limited-speed motorcycle, or moped, you must sign the declaration on the M2 Examination form stating that your limited-speed motorcycle, or moped is capable of maintaining a safe speed on a 50 km/h road. The safe speed may vary depending on road and traffic conditions. If you are unable to sign the declaration, your road test will be cancelled and you may be charged half of your test fee.

During the M2 road test, the examiner will give you directions through a disposable earphone and, as you complete the tasks, will watch to make sure you successfully perform the required skills.

When you book a road test, you will be required to indicate the type of vehicle you plan to bring to the test (for example, motorcycle, limited-speed motorcycle, or moped). The type of motorcycle you bring to the test will determine the type of licence you will receive.

If you pass the road test on a motorcycle that is not three-wheeled or limited-speed, you get a class M licence and you may drive a two-wheeled or three-wheeled motorcycle on any public road in Ontario. You may also drive a limited-speed motorcycle, or moped, on public roads other than those listed in Regulation 630 of the *Highway Traffic Act*.

If you pass the test on a limited-speed motorcycle, or moped, you get an M(L) licence and you may drive a limited-speed motorcycle, or moped, on public roads other than controlled-access highways and those roads listed in Regulation 630 of the *Highway Traffic Act*.

If you pass the test on a three-wheeled motorcycle, you get an M (M) licence, which allows you to only drive motor tricycles on public roads.

Please note: For a complete listing of public roads prohibited to limited-speed motorcycles and mopeds, please see Regulation 630 of the *Highway Traffic Act* at www.e-laws.gov.on.ca. You should also be aware that municipalities may pass bylaws prohibiting limited-speed motorcycles and mopeds on municipal roads with speeds of 80 km/h or greater.

Level Two road test - checklist

Bring the following items to the test:
• Vehicle in good working order (see "Out-of-order road test" on page 16)
• Motorcycle helmet
• Current driver's licence
• Money for test fees (if applicable)
• Glasses or contact lenses (if you need to wear them to drive)

Arrive at least 30 minutes before the road test appointment.

Remember: If you take your road test as part of a ministry-approved motorcycle safety course, your course certificate is valid for only six months. Be sure to take it to a DriveTest Centre before the six months have passed or you will have to take your road test over again.

Upgrading from class M(L) or class M(M) to class M

If you already hold an M2(L), M(L), M2(M) or M(M) licence and you want to upgrade to a full-class M licence (no L or M condition), you must pass both road tests on a motor-cycle that is not a three-wheeled or a limited-speed motorcycle. You must first obtain a 90-day motorcycle training TDL (temporary driver's licence), available from the Queen's Park Driver and Vehicle Licence Issuing Office or any DriveTest Centre. This TDL allows you to practise driving a non-three-wheeled or a non-limited-speed motorcycle. You need this TDL to take the required road test(s) as well.

For more information on road tests, see chapters 8 and 9 of this handbook.

Out-of-order road test

If your vehicle does not meet ministry standards for the purpose of a road test, or if there is a non-vehicle-related reason for which the examiner determines that the road test cannot be completed, the examiner declares the road test out-of-order. You lose 50 per cent of your road test fee. The other 50 per cent of the fee remains as a credit on your driving record, and may be applied when booking a new road test. In order to book the new road test, you will have to pay the 50 per cent of the fee lost through the out-of-order.

You must bring the appropriate vehicle to the road test you have booked. For example, if you have booked a regular motorcycle road test, you cannot bring a limited-speed motorcycle. If you do bring a limited-speed motorcycle, and the DriveTest Centre cannot accommodate a limited-speed road test that day, your road test will be declared out of order, and you will lose

50 per cent of the fee. You will have to rebook your test.

If you have any concerns that your road test may be declared out-of-order, contact the DriveTest Centre before your scheduled test to discuss it.

Visitors and new Ontario residents

If you are a visitor to Ontario and want to drive while you are here, you must be at least 16 years old and have a valid motorcycle licence from your own province, state or country.

If you are from another country and visiting Ontario for more than three months, you need an international driver's permit from your own country. If you do not have an international driver's permit, you can apply for an Ontario licence.

If you are a new resident of Ontario and have a valid motorcycle licence from another province or country, you can use that licence

for 60 days in Ontario. If you want to continue to drive after 60 days, you must get an Ontario motorcycle licence.

New residents from Australia, Canada, Northern Ireland, Switzerland and the United States

If you are a licensed motorcycle driver (of motorcycles other than limited-speed motorcycles or motor tricycles) with two or more years of driving experience in the last three years in another Canadian province or territory, Australia, Northern Ireland, Switzerland or the United States, you may get full-class M licence privileges without taking a knowledge or road test.

If you are a licensed limited-speed motorcycle, or moped, driver from Saskatchewan, New Brunswick, Prince Edward Island or Quebec, you are eligible for a full-class M(L) licence without taking a knowledge or road test.

In either case, you must meet all medical requirements, including a vision test, and show acceptable proof of your previous licence status and driving experience. If you have less than two years of driving experience in the last three years, you may get credit for your experience and enter Level Two of the graduated licensing system. Once you have a total of two years driving experience, you may take the Level Two road test to earn full driving privileges.

New residents from other areas

If you are a licensed motorcycle or moped driver from a country other than Canada, the United States or Switzerland, you must pass a vision test and a written test of your knowledge of motorcycles and the rules of the road. You must also pass a written test of your knowledge of traffic signs.

If you have acceptable proof of two or more years of driving experience, you may take the Level Two road test to earn full driving privileges. If you do not pass this road test, you will get a Level One licence and may immediately schedule a Level One road test.

If you have less than two years of driving experience, you will be placed in Level One. However, if you have acceptable proof that you have the driving experience required for Level One, you can immediately schedule a Level One road test. A motorcycle licence from another area is considered acceptable proof if it shows you have the driving experience required. If you do not have such a motorcycle licence to show as proof of your driving experience, you must start at the beginning of Level One as a new driver.

Chapter 1 - Summary
By the end of this chapter, you should know:
- The differences between a motorcycle, a motor tricycle, a limited-speed motorcycle, or a moped
- The requirements to drive a motorcycle or moped under the Graduated Licensing System
- General information on the Level One and Level Two road tests
- What to bring to a knowledge or road test
- What may result in an out-of-order road test
- How to obtain a motorcycle licence if you were previously licensed in another jurisdiction

COULD YOU PASS?

The rest of this handbook gives you information you will need to pass your tests and keep your driving privileges once you get your motorcycle licence. Here is a sample question that could appear on the written knowledge test:

When a group of motorcyclists is travelling together, the safest way to drive is: (choose one)
 A. Staggered formation
 B. Four side by side
 C. Three side by side
 D. In a group

The knowledge test may also ask you about:
• Rules of the road
• Traffic signs
• Knowledge of motorcycle controls
• Proper lane position
• Steering control of a motorcycle
• Motorcycle equipment requirements
• Safety helmets
• Carrying passengers or cargo

• Handling dangerous surfaces
• Downshifting of gears
• Proper maintenance of
  your motorcycle

The road tests will test how well you use your knowledge. You will be tested on:
• Starting, stopping and turning
• Traffic signs and lights
• Passing vehicles and driving in
  passing lanes
• Travelling through controlled and
  uncontrolled intersections
• Entering and exiting freeways (not
  applicable to road tests taken on
  limited-speed motorcycles, or mopeds)
• Foreseeing hazardous conditions
  and being ready for them
• Other safe driving practices

Make sure you read and understand the information in this handbook and The *Official MTO Driver's Handbook* **before you take your tests.**

CHAPTER 2
GETTING READY TO DRIVE

This chapter tells you how to get yourself and your motorcycle or moped ready to drive. This includes being in good physical and mental condition; wearing a helmet and the proper clothing; knowing your vehicle and its controls; and making sure your vehicle is safe to drive.

Get into the right frame of mind

Driving a motorcycle or moped is different from driving a car or any other kind of vehicle. It takes your full concentration and attention to remain safe and in control. This means that you need to be in good physical and mental condition. Do not drive when you are sick, injured, tired, upset or impaired in any way. You need to be calm, alert and focused every time you drive.

Avoid drugs and alcohol

Drinking alcohol increases your chances of having a collision. Alcohol can begin to affect your ability to handle your motorcycle safely at blood-alcohol levels far below the legal limit. Your balance, steering, speed control and distance perception may be off. Because alcohol also clouds your judgment, you may not recognize these symptoms of impairment until it is too late.

Besides alcohol, almost any drug can affect your ability to drive a vehicle safely. This includes illegal and prescription drugs. It even includes non-prescription drugs such as cold tablets or allergy pills. These drugs can leave you weak, dizzy or drowsy. Make sure you know the effects of any drug before you drive. If you feel dizzy or weak while driving, stop and wait until you feel normal.

Read chapter 4, "Keeping your driver's licence," in the *Official MTO Driver's Handbook*, to understand the consequences of driving while impaired.

Cell phones

Cell phones can be an important safety aid for drivers, but using a cell phone while driving takes a driver's attention away from the task of driving and increases the risk of collision. Viewing display screens unrelated to driving is prohibited while driving. Distracted drivers are more likely to make mistakes or react too slowly. A **fully licensed driver** or a **hybrid driver** who talks, texts, types, dials or e-mails using hand-held cellular phones and other hand-held communications and entertainment devices faces fines of up to $1,000 and three demerit points applied to their driver's record under Ontario's distracted driving law. A novice driver (subject to the graduated licensing program) convicted of distracted driving will be subject to escalating sanctions.

Police can also charge drivers with careless driving or even dangerous driving (a criminal offence) if they do not pay full attention to the driving task.

Stay calm and alert

Do not drive when you are tired. You might fall asleep while driving, risking your own life and the lives of others on the road. Even if you do not fall asleep, fatigue affects your ability to perceive and react to emergencies.Your thinking slows down and you miss seeing things. In an emergency, you may make the wrong decision or you may not make the right one fast enough. It is also important not to drive when you are upset or angry. Strong emotions can reduce your ability to think and react quickly. Be especially careful not to fall victim to road rage, or you could find yourself in a vulnerable and dangerous position.

Wear a helmet

A helmet is the most important motorcycle or moped accessory you can have. Wearing a helmet can protect you from serious head injury. Ontario law requires you and your passenger to wear approved helmets with the chin strap securely fastened every time you drive a motorcycle or moped.

An approved helmet is one that meets standards approved for use in Ontario. It must have a strong chin strap and fastener, and be in good condition. Approved helmets come in a variety of styles and prices. It is important to choose one that is well constructed and will protect you. A full-faced helmet offers the best protection and the most comfort. A helmet with bright colours

and reflective devices may make you more visible to other drivers.

Make sure your helmet fits snugly and does not slide around on your head. Always keep the strap securely fastened. Studies of motorcycle collisions show that a loose helmet will come off in a collision.

Besides protecting you from head injury, a helmet can make you more comfortable when driving because it reduces the noise of the road and keeps the wind, bugs and other debris from blowing in your face.

Wear protective clothing

Protective clothing can help protect you from injury in a fall or collision and from the impact of wind, rain, insects, stones and debris. It can also help reduce fatigue by keeping you warm in bad weather. Bright colours and reflective items, such as a safety vest, make you more visible to other drivers on the road.

Wear a jacket and pants that cover your arms and legs completely, even in warm weather. Leather offers the best protection, but riding suits made of special synthetic materials, can also give you a lot of protection.

Your clothes should fit snugly enough to keep from flapping but still let you move freely. Consider wearing protective equipment such as back protectors, kidney belts and body armour as inserts in your protective clothing.

In cold or wet weather, your clothes should keep you warm and dry as well as protect you from injury. Driving for long periods in cold weather can cause severe chill and fatigue. Rain suits should be one piece and brightly coloured. Those not designed for motorcycle use may balloon out and allow wind and water to enter when driving at freeway speeds. A winter jacket should resist wind and fit snugly at neck, wrists and waist. Layer your clothes for extra warmth and protection.

Choose boots that are sturdy and high enough to protect your ankles. Soles should be made of hard, durable material that will grip the pavement when you are stopped. Heels should be short so they will not catch on rough surfaces. Avoid shoes with rings or laces that may catch on the motorcycle's controls.

Gloves are also important in both cold and warm weather. They give you a better hold on the hand-grips and controls. Gauntlet gloves that extend over your wrists are recommended because they protect your wrists, as well as your fingers and knuckles. Look for sturdy leather gloves designed for motorcycle use.

Know your vehicle

The first step in learning to drive a motorcycle or moped is to learn where the controls are and what they do. Motorcycles and mopeds are designed so that all the controls are within quick reach of your hands and feet. However, the same control may not be in the same place on all vehicles. Also, some types of mopeds have different controls than motorcycles. Become familiar with your vehicle's controls. Check the owner's manual for the exact location and precise method of operation of all controls.

You need to know the controls well enough that you can reach them without taking your eyes off the road. With practice, you will be able to operate all controls by reflex. This automatic response is required before you can begin to drive in traffic.

Primary controls

The following six controls are the most important controls you will use to operate your motorcycle or moped:

1. Handlebars
2. Throttle
3. Front brake lever
4. Rear brake lever
5. Clutch lever
6. Shift lever

This illustration is intended only as a guide. Controls and their positions may be different on your vehicle. Some motorcycles and mopeds do not have clutch or shift levers.

1. Handlebars

These are the two bars you hold to control the motorcycle's direction. Many of the other controls are grouped on or around the handlebars.

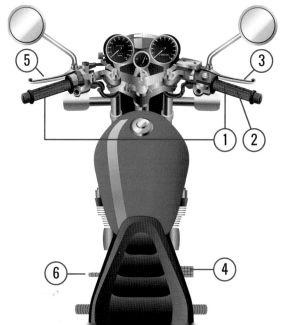

2. Throttle

Twist the right handgrip to operate the throttle. This controls the motorcycle's speed by controlling the flow of fuel to the engine. To speed up, twist the throttle toward you. To slow down, twist it away from you. The throttle should spring back completely to the idle position when you let go.

3. Front brake lever

The front brake lever is on the right handlebar in front of the throttle. You squeeze the lever toward the handgrip to apply the brake to the front wheel. Use the front and rear brakes together.

4. Rear brake lever

The rear brake lever is near the right foot rest. Press your foot on the lever to apply the brake to the rear wheel. Use the front and rear brakes together.

If your motorcycle has a clutch and gears, remember that although the engine will act as a brake when you gear down or reduce throttle, your brake lights will not turn on and other drivers may not know you are slowing down. Always apply your brakes as a signal to others that you are slowing down.

5. Clutch lever

The clutch lever is on the left handle-bar. It controls the clutch and is used to help shift gears. Squeeze the lever toward the handgrip to disengage the clutch; release it to engage the clutch. Whenever you change gears, you must first disengage the clutch. Try to co-ordinate the movements of clutch and throttle to change gears smoothly.

Most limited-speed motorcycles and mopeds have an automatic clutch lever.

6. Shift lever

The shift lever is near the left foot-rest. It shifts the transmission's gears. The shift lever should only be used when the clutch is disengaged. Select the gear you need by lifting or pressing the lever with your foot. Most motorcycles have five or six forward gears and a neutral position. Always start and shut off your motorcycle in neutral.

Most limited-speed motorcycles and all mopeds have automatic gear shifting.

Secondary controls

There are a number of secondary controls that you will need to use to operate a motorcycle or moped effectively. Here are some of the most important ones:

7. Speedometer
8. Tachometer
9. Indicator lights
10. Ignition switch
11. Starter
12. Choke
13. Engine kill switch
14. Fuel-supply valve
15. Turn signals switch
16. Horn button
17. Light switches
18. Stands

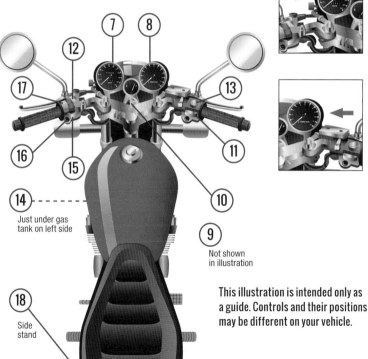

14
Just under gas
tank on left side

9
Not shown
in illustration

18
Side
stand

This illustration is intended only as a guide. Controls and their positions may be different on your vehicle.

7. Speedometer

The speedometer shows the speed you are driving in kilometres per hour or miles per hour.

8. Tachometer

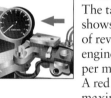

The tachometer shows the number of revolutions your engine is turning per minute (rpm). A red line shows the maximum rpm that is safe for the engine.

9. Indicator lights

The high-beam light glows red or blue when the highbeam headlight is on. The neutral light glows green when the transmission is in neutral gear. And the turn signal light flashes yellow when the left or right turn signal is on.

10. Ignition switch

The ignition switch turns the ignition system on and off. The ignition switch is separate from the starter; you do not turn the key to start a motorcycle like you do a car. Ignition switches have "on" and "off" positions and some also have "lights," "lock" and "park" positions.

11. Starter

Most motorcycles have electric starters. To start, make sure your motorcycle is in neutral and that the clutch is depressed. Push the starter button on the right handlebar near the throttle. Some motorcycles have a kick-start lever, usually above the right footrest. It must be unfolded and kicked downward to start the motorcycle.

Most mopeds require you to pedal in order to start the engine.

12. Choke

This is a lever or knob, usually on the handlebars, that is used to help start the motorcycle by adjusting the mixture of gasoline and air supplied to the engine. It is used when starting a cold engine.

13. Engine kill switch

The engine kill switch is used in an emergency to stop the engine quickly. It may also be used to turn off the engine after a normal stop, but be sure to turn off the ignition switch as well. The engine will not start when the kill switch is in the "off" position.

Some older model motorcycles and mopeds do not have a kill switch.

14. Fuel-supply valve

The fuel supply may be controlled by a manually operated valve, or petcock, which controls the flow of gasoline to the engine. When the vehicle is not in use, this valve should be turned off to avoid a fire hazard. The fuel tank may also have a manually selected reserve supply in case the main section runs dry. To release the reserve fuel, you must turn the valve to reserve.

Many newer model motorcycles do not have manual fuel-control valves.

15. Turn signals switch

Many motorcycle and moped turn signals do not automatically switch off after a turn is completed. You must manually switch off the signal after each turn or lane change. Forgetting to turn off your signal is as dangerous as not signalling in the first place, because it may cause other drivers to pull out or turn in front of you.

16. Horn button

Your motorcycle or moped must have a horn that works. Most horns are operated by pushing a button with your thumb.

17. Light switches

On most modern motorcycles and mopeds, the headlight and tail light come on automatically when the ignition is switched on and the engine is running. The switch to turn the headlight from low beam to high beam is usually on the left handlebar and operated by the thumb.

18. Stands

A kickstand or centre stand holds a motorcycle or moped upright when it is parked. Some larger motorcycles have both a kickstand and a centre stand. A kickstand extends from the left side of the vehicle and the vehicle leans against it. A centre stand is attached underneath the centre of the frame and holds the vehicle upright. Stands are operated by spring mechanisms and should only be used on a hard surface. Always make sure to completely raise your stands before driving away.

DO A PRE-DRIVE VEHICLE CHECK

Motorcycles and mopeds require more attention and upkeep than cars, since the consequences of something going wrong are usually much more severe when on a motorcycle than while driving a car. You should always check the condition of the vehicle before you drive it. Here are the things you should check every time before you drive a motorcycle or moped:

Tires

The proper tires are important for good traction, mileage and safety. Check your tires for the following:

- **Pressure** – Proper tire pressure means safer driving and longer-lasting tires. Use an air-pressure gauge to check the pressure when the tires are cold. If you do not know what your tire pressure should be, check the owner's manual or with the manufacturer.

- **Tread** – Worn or uneven tread can make the vehicle skid, particularly on wet pavement.
- **Damage** – Check for cuts or nails stuck in the tread. Also, check for wear, bulges or cracking. A blowout on a motorcycle can be extremely dangerous.

Controls

Make sure all levers, pedals and switches are in good condition and operate properly. They should spring back to the original position when you let go.

Brakes

Try the front and rear brakes one at a time. Make sure each one holds the motorcycle or moped when it is fully applied. It is especially important to test the brakes of a motorcycle or moped you are unfamiliar with or have never ridden before.

Chassis

Check for loose bolts.

Cables

Check for kinks, binding or broken strands.

Lights

The headlight(s) must shine a white light. The rear or tail light(s) must be red. A white light must shine on the licence plate. Keep your lights clean and check that all are working before you drive away.

Fuel and oil

Check levels.

Stands

Check springs.

Adjust your mirrors

Clean and adjust both mirrors before you start. It is dangerous to try to adjust a mirror while driving. Swing mirrors outward far enough to see around your own body. Adjust each mirror so that it lets you see about half the lane behind you and as much of the lane beside you as possible. Reduce your blind spot as much as possible. If your motorcycle or moped has convex mirrors, note that convex mirrors make other vehicles look farther away than they really are. Remember that checking your mirrors is not a substitute for looking over your shoulder.

Turn on your headlight

All motorcycles must have a white light at the front (headlight) and a red light at the back (rear or tail light) and these must be used at all times of day and night.

When driving a moped, headlights and tail lights (or a rear reflector) are required to be used between one-half hour before sunset and one-half hour after sunrise, and any other time of poor light conditions, such as fog, snow or rain, which keeps you from clearly seeing people or vehicles less than 150 metres away. It is recommended that your moped's full lighting system be turned on at all times to enhance your safety and the safety of others. In addition, mopeds are required to have white reflective material on the front forks and red reflective material on the back forks.

Chapter 2 - Summary
By the end of this chapter, you should know:
- The importance of being mentally and physically prepared to drive
- The type of helmet and protective clothing to wear when riding
- The primary and secondary controls of a motorcycle and how to operate them
- Motorcycle components to be checked before every trip
- How to use your mirrors and headlight for optimal vision and visibility

CHAPTER 3
BASIC MOTORCYCLE AND MOPED DRIVING SKILLS

This chapter tells you about the basic skills you need to drive a motorcycle or moped. Controlling your motorcycle or moped means being able to make it go exactly where you want and at the correct speed. It will take practice and experience to master the basic skills of starting, steering, turning, shifting gears and stopping. Practise off the road, in a parking lot or other spot away from traffic, until you can perform all the manoeuvres safely and confidently.

Take a motorcycle safety course
The best way to learn proper motorcycle driving techniques right from the start is to take a motorcycle safety course. You will learn good driving habits from trained instructors, increasing your chances of a safe and enjoyable driving experience. There are also safety courses available for limited-speed motorcycles. For more information on how to find a motorcycle safety course and what you will learn, see page 90, or visit the Ministry of Transportation website at www.mto.gov.on.ca.

Getting on the motorcycle or moped
Begin by making sure your vehicle is not too heavy or large for you to drive comfortably. Sitting on the seat, you should be able to place your feet flat on the ground.

If your motorcycle or moped has a kickstand, mount the vehicle from the left side and straighten it with the handlebars. With the vehicle balanced, use your left heel to kick the stand up and out of the way.

If your motorcycle or moped is resting on a centre stand, mount the vehicle and gently rock it forward until it rolls off the stand. The centre stand will spring into the "up" position. Stop the vehicle from continuing to roll forward by applying the front brake.

Always make sure to completely raise your kickstand and centre stand before driving away.

Starting your motorcycle

Depending on the age and model of your motorcycle, the starting procedure may vary. Generally, you start a motorcycle (not a limited-speed motorcycle) by turning the ignition switch on and making sure the engine kill switch is not in the "off" position. (This can happen by accident, so it is always a good idea to check.)

Shift your transmission into neutral. Set your choke as required.

(How you do this will depend on whether your engine is cold, as well as the individual characteristics of your vehicle.) Pull in the clutch and press the starter button. Release the button as soon as you hear the engine fire. If your motorcycle has a kick-starter instead of an electric starter, you will need to unfold the lever, usually above the right footrest, and kick it downward to start the motorcycle.

Once the engine is going, shift into first gear and, with your feet still on the ground, slowly ease the clutch lever out until the motorcycle begins to move forward. Raise your feet and continue to ease up on the clutch, applying the throttle to give the engine enough fuel not to stall.

Starting your limited-speed motorcycle, or moped

Most modern limited-speed motorcycles have a type of automatic transmission called a continuously variable transmission, and start automatically when you turn the ignition key. Most mopeds are started by pedalling first, then turning the ignition key. You must consult your operator's manual and learn the proper starting technique for your vehicle.

Using clutch controls and shifting gears (if applicable)

If your motorcycle is equipped with a clutch and gears, shift gears as you increase and decrease engine speed — shift up when driving faster and shift down when slowing down.

The purpose of the gears in a motorcycle transmission is to match the engine's speed (measured by the tachometer) with the motorcycle's speed (measured by the speedometer). The proper gear will also provide power for the motorcycle to accelerate if necessary.

Learning to co-ordinate the movements of the clutch and throttle to change gears smoothly is a critically important part of driving. Make sure you can accelerate and decelerate smoothly before you attempt to drive in traffic.

To shift up, twist the throttle as you pull in the clutch. Move the shift lever up with your toe until it stops. When you can hear and feel the gear engage, ease off on the clutch and slowly twist the throttle back up to speed.

It is more difficult to downshift smoothly than to shift up. You must twist the throttle slightly to increase engine speed as you downshift with the clutch pulled in. If you do not apply enough throttle, the motorcycle may jerk when you release the clutch. To avoid a rear-wheel skid, downshift when the engine speed is lower than the motorcycle's speed.

Do not shift gears while you are turning. A rough, jerky downshift can cause the rear wheel to lock, resulting in a skid. Applying too much power can cause the rear tire to lose traction, also resulting in a skid. It is best to shift gears before entering a turn.

Remember: You shift up when the engine is turning too fast for the motorcycle's speed or to increase speed, and you downshift when the engine is turning too slowly or you want to slow down.

Driving along

Steering a motorcycle or moped is very different from steering a car. When driving a motorcycle or moped, you must use your entire body to control the balance and steering of your vehicle.

Driving along, your body posture should be fairly straight. Sit close enough to the handlebars to reach them with your arms slightly bent so that you can turn the handlebars without having to stretch. Hold the handgrips firmly enough that you will not lose your grip if the motorcycle or moped bounces. Drive with your wrists low to keep you from increasing your speed by mistake. Hold your knees firmly against the gas tank for comfort and better control. To maintain your balance, keep your feet firmly on the footrests. Do not drag your foot along the ground. Keep your toes up so they do not get caught between the road surface and the footrest.

Keep your motorcycle or moped as vertical as possible, especially when accelerating.

Turning
You need to be extra careful when turning or changing lanes on a motorcycle or moped. The only way to learn how to make good, precise turns is to practise.

Slow down before entering a turn. Approach turns with extra caution until you learn to judge how fast you can actually take a turn. If you cannot hold a turn, you may end up crossing into another lane of traffic or going off the road.

If you brake too hard when turning, you may skid out of control. Check your mirrors and

over your shoulder to be sure the way is clear, and signal well in advance to alert other drivers that you intend to turn or change lanes. Then lean with the vehicle into the turn. The sharper the turn and the faster your speed, the more you lean. Look well ahead in your turn. Practise keeping your head upright and facing into the turn. Remember, slow down before you begin to turn. And speed up to come out of the turn. To keep control of your steering, avoid braking in the turn.

Braking and stopping
The front brake is the more important of the two brakes; it provides about three-quarters of your stopping power. However, you must use both front and rear brakes to slow down and stop effectively. Be careful not to apply the brakes too hard; you may lock up your tires and skid. Here are some tips for braking and stopping properly:

Always
- If your vehicle has gears, gear down during deceleration to a gear appropriate to your speed.
- Use all your fingers to pull the front brake lever smoothly.
- Apply both front and rear brakes every time you slow down or stop.
- Apply both brakes at the same time.
- When braking hard, keep the motorcycle or moped as vertical as possible.

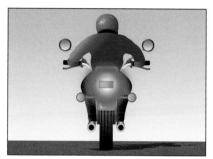

- Stop in the appropriate tire track to block the lane.
- If behind a large vehicle, stop where its driver is still able to see you in the driver-side mirror.
- Do all your braking before you enter a turn.
- When stopped, keep both brakes on and keep your left foot on the ground.

Remember: You can also slow down by downshifting or reducing throttle. However, your brake lights will not turn on when you do this, so other drivers may not know you are slowing down. Always apply your brakes as a signal to others that you are slowing down.

Never
- Rely solely on gearing down to bring your vehicle to a stop.
- Weave your motorcycle or moped to slow down.
- Drag your foot when coming to a stop.
- Balance at a low speed instead of coming to a complete stop.

Parking your motorcycle or moped
When parking your motorcycle or moped, use your foot to push the kickstand down. Carefully lean the vehicle to the left to rest on the kickstand.

If your motorcycle or moped has a centre stand, follow these steps to park it:
1. Stand beside the left side of the motorcycle or moped and hold onto both handgrips.

2. Using your right foot, lower the centre stand until you feel it touch the ground.
3. Balance the vehicle upright and use one hand to grasp the frame under the saddle.
4. With your right foot securely placed on the centre stand, push down and back on the stand with your foot while pulling the motorcycle back with your arms. The vehicle should roll up onto the centre stand.

Chapter 3 - Summary

By the end of this chapter, you should know:

- How to get on, start, turn, brake and park your motorcycle or moped
- The proper body position and method to shift gears

CHAPTER 4
SAFE AND RESPONSIBLE DRIVING

Driving defensively

Driving a motorcycle or moped in traffic is more dangerous than driving a car or truck. That is why it is so important to learn the basic skills of driving before you attempt driving in traffic. When driving in traffic, you will need to focus all your attention on what you are seeing and hearing, and then judging what is going to happen next.

This chapter tells you about the most important principles of safe and responsible driving. These include seeing and being seen; clearly communicating with other drivers; keeping a cushion of space around your motorcycle for safety; and positioning yourself in the best possible spot on the road. Together these strategies are the basis for what is called defensive driving or strategic driving.

I. VISIBILITY

Seeing

The best way to avoid trouble is to see it coming. Skilled drivers have very few surprises on the road because they see and understand possible problems before getting to them. Learn to look far ahead of where you are driving. In the city, look one-half to one full block ahead. On the freeway, look as far ahead as you can see. Looking well ahead gives you time to adjust to problems. It also helps you to avoid panic stops or sudden swerves that can cause even more trouble.

Follow these steps to develop driver awareness:

- Keep your eyes constantly moving and scanning the road ahead, beside and behind. Do not look at one place for more than two seconds; trouble could be developing while you are not looking.
- Look ahead as far as you can see. Look beyond the vehicle in front of you for others that are stopping or turning ahead.
- Check the roadside. Watch for vehicles that may leave the curb or enter from side streets or driveways.

Sometimes you cannot see an area because a bridge or truck blocks your view. Good drivers have good imaginations. Ask yourself what might be there that you cannot see yet. Remember, what you cannot see can hurt you.

When looking ahead and scanning the road, check the surface of the road for slippery spots, bumps, broken pavement, loose gravel, wet leaves or objects lying in the road. When driving in winter, be alert for ice and snow patches. Learn to see these spots well ahead so you do not have to look down at the road surface.

In some situations, you can put your motorcycle in a position to see things that other drivers cannot. For example, in a blind curve, where you cannot see all the way around, move to the side of the lane where you can see as much as possible of the road ahead.

At blind intersections, after stopping, ease forward past obstructions to see if anything is coming.

When you are parked or stopped at the side of the road and want to join traffic, angle your motorcycle across the road so that you can see in both directions.

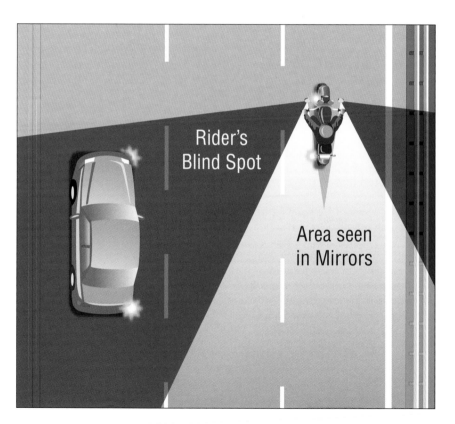

Rider's Blind Spot

Area seen in Mirrors

Check your mirrors

Check your mirrors every five to seven seconds to keep track of traffic coming up behind you. You should have a good picture in your mind of what is behind so someone passing you will not surprise you. You also need to know in order to stop quickly or swerve if necessary.

It is especially important to check your mirrors in the following situations:

- **Before you have to slow down or stop suddenly or when you are stopped at an intersection.** If the driver behind you is not paying attention, she or he may be dangerously close before noticing you are there. Be prepared to get out of the way.

- **Before you make a turn.**
Check vehicles behind you when
you plan to slow down and turn.
Remember to use your brake
lights to signal that you are slowing
down. (Gearing down does
not activate your brake lights.)
If drivers behind you do not
appear to be aware that you
are turning, it may be safer
to continue going straight.
- **Before you change lanes.**
Make sure no one is trying
to pass you.

Remember that mirrors do not give
the whole traffic picture. There is an
area on each side of your motorcycle
or moped that you cannot see in
your mirror. You may not see people
or vehicles when they are in these
blind spots. Always turn your head
and check over your shoulder
before you turn or change lanes.

Being seen

You cannot assume that other
drivers see you. Drivers who have
collided with motorcycles often
say they did not see the motorcycle
until it was too late.

A motorcycle or moped is
more difficult to see than other
vehicles. Your profile is smaller
from most angles. Even if you are
seen, your speed or distance from
other vehicles may be misjudged.
If a driver does not see you, she or
he may pull out or turn in front of
you or cut you off. Always ask
yourself if the other driver sees you.

Even when other drivers see
you, you may be hit if they misjudge
your speed, are aggressive or
impaired, or just careless. Be alert
and try to anticipate what other
drivers are likely to do.

While your motorcycle or
moped's headlight(s) and tail light(s)
help to make you visible, there are a
number of other things you can do to
increase your visibility:
- **Wear brightly coloured clothing
and helmet.** This will help make
you more visible during the day,
especially from angles where
your headlight cannot be seen.
Yellow, orange, red and other
bright colours are highly visible.
Black and dark colours are not.
Think about wearing a reflective
vest, especially at night. Consider
adding reflective tape to your
helmet, clothing and vehicle. In
the rain, wear reflective rainwear.

- **Slow down when driving at night in front of a group of vehicles.** When you are driving in traffic with other headlights behind you, a driver ahead may not be able to pick out your single light from all the lights behind you. This problem is especially bad when the roads are wet because of lights reflecting off the road surface.

- **Think about your lane position.** Sometimes you can make yourself more visible by moving from one side of the lane to the other or by changing lanes when appropriate.

Do not drive in another driver's blind spot, and do not let another vehicle drive in your blind spot. Drop back or pass the other driver. When you pass another vehicle, get through the blind spot as soon as you can. Approach cautiously but, once you are alongside, get by quickly. As a general rule, if you can see a driver in his or her mirror, the driver can see you.

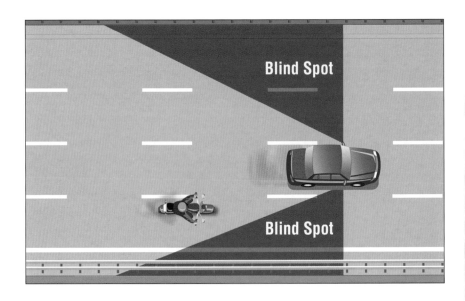

Being seen at intersections

Most collisions between motorcycles or mopeds and other vehicles happen at intersections. The two leading causes of these collisions are: 1) drivers often have a hard time seeing a motorcycle or moped coming toward them; and 2) a vehicle may make a left turn across your path or pull out from a side street. To cut down your chances of being hit, follow these steps:

- **Approach slowly.** If a driver does pull out suddenly, your chances of making a quick stop or a quick turn are better if you are going slowly.
- **Move as far away as you can from the other vehicle.** If the vehicle is on your right, move to the left. For a vehicle on your left or an oncoming vehicle with a left-turn signal on, move to the right.

- **Move away from things that could block the other driver's view.** When you approach an intersection with a vehicle waiting to pull out, move toward the centre of the road so that you are in the other driver's line of sight.

Chapter 4, Section I - Summary
By the end of this section, you should know:
- How and where to look when you are driving along
- How to use your mirrors to see behind you in a variety of situations
- How to make yourself more visible to other road users

II. COMMUNICATING WITH OTHER DRIVERS

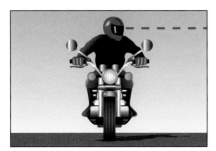

In addition to seeing and being seen, it is important to communicate with other drivers to make sure they see you and know what you are doing. Make eye contact with other drivers. Check over your shoulder often to make sure other drivers are not crowding you.

Be ready to use your horn, if necessary, before you pass a vehicle, or approach a driveway or intersection where a vehicle may pull out in front of you. You can use your horn before passing a vehicle you think might move into your lane. Watch for situations such as a driver in the lane next to you coming up behind a vehicle; a parked car with someone in it; or someone walking or riding a bicycle on the road.

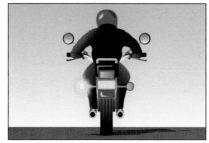

Use your signals to communicate. A driver behind you is more likely to understand your turn signal than your tail light. Use your turn signals even when what you plan to do is obvious. For example, if you use your signals on a freeway entrance ramp, it is more likely that vehicles on the freeway will see you and make room for you. Also, signal whenever you change lanes whether someone else is around or not. It is when you do not see the other vehicle that your signals are most important.

Remember to turn off your signal after you have completed your turn or lane change. It can be as dangerous to forget to turn a signal off as it is to forget to turn it on. A driver may think that you plan to turn or make a lane change. Check your instrument panel to see if you have left a signal on. If you have an older model vehicle that did not come with turn signals, use the standard hand and arm signals as

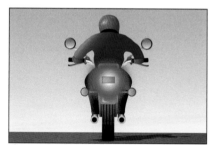

shown in the diagrams here. This also applies if your turn signals or brake lights are not working, in which case you should proceed to take your vehicle off the road until repairs can be made. Manual hand and arm signals are less effective during poor light conditions and may not be visible to others. Exercise extra caution if your turn signals and brake lights are not working.

When watching for signals made by others, remember that cyclists may signal right turns by holding their right arm straight out.

Tap the brake pedal lightly to flash your brake light before you slow

Left Turn

Right Turn

Slowing Down OR Stopping

down. This warns drivers behind you that you are going to slow

down. This is especially important when you are being followed too closely, when you are making a tight turn off a high-speed road, or when you are slowing down or turning where others may not expect it. Also, keep your foot on the brake, day or night, when stopped for a stop sign or traffic signal.

Chapter 4, Section II - Summary
By the end of this section, you should know:
- How to use eye contact and your horn to communicate with other road users
- How to use signals and brake lights to communicate your intentions to other road users

III. KEEP A CUSHION OF SPACE AROUND YOU

The best protection you have as a motorcycle or moped driver is distance between you and other drivers. Distance gives you time to react to trouble and find some place to move if necessary.

Always leave a cushion of space around your vehicle to let other drivers see you and to avoid a collision. Keep alert for all other traffic, including vehicles in front, behind, coming toward you and approaching from the side, as well as those you are passing and any that are passing you.

It is important to remember that motorcycles and mopeds, because they weigh less than most other vehicles on the road, are able to stop and accelerate faster than other vehicles. Keep in mind when deciding how much space to leave around you that other drivers may need much more space to stop than you do.

Distance in front

Always keep at least a two-second distance behind the vehicle in front of you. This gives you time to react if something happens ahead. It also gives you a better view of things in the road, such as potholes, slippery spots, chunks of tire tread or debris. If conditions are less than ideal, such as in bad weather, leave even more space. To give yourself at least a two-second space, follow these steps:

1. Pick a marker on the road ahead, such as a road sign or hydro pole.
2. When the rear of the vehicle ahead passes the marker, count "one thousand and one, one thousand and two."
3. When you reach the marker, stop counting. If you reach the marker before you count "one thousand and two," you are following too closely.

2 Seconds or More

When you stop behind another vehicle, leave enough space to pull out and pass without having to back up about one motorcycle length. If the vehicle in front is large, leave more space. Leaving this space protects you in three ways: it lets you pull around the vehicle in front if it stalls; it helps prevent you from being pushed into the vehicle ahead if you are hit from behind; and it reduces the risk of collision if the vehicle ahead rolls backward or backs up.

Distance to the side

On a motorcycle or moped, you have the ability to change your position within the lane to increase your distance from other vehicles. You should do this as traffic conditions change.

Try to keep a space on both sides of your vehicle. Do not drive beside other vehicles if you can avoid it. A vehicle in the next lane could move into your lane without warning. Vehicles in the next lane also block your escape if you run into danger in your lane. Drop back or speed up until you find a place that is clear on both sides. Avoid driving in other drivers' blind spots.

The following are some of the conditions that require changes in lane position:

- **Passing vehicles**
  When you are being passed by an oncoming vehicle or from behind, move toward the centre of the lane.

Avoid being closer to a passing vehicle than you have to be; a slight mistake by either driver could cause a sideswipe.

- **Parked vehicles**
  By staying to the left side of the lane, you can avoid the dangers of opening doors, drivers getting out of vehicles or people stepping from between vehicles.
- **Vehicles pulling out**
  When pulling out into traffic, other drivers often take a quick look behind them and fail to see a motorcycle or moped. Vehicles making U-turns are a particular danger. If you see a vehicle pulling out, approach with caution.

Distance behind

Many drivers complain about "tailgaters" — people who follow others too closely. If someone is following you too closely, change lanes and let the tailgater pass. If a driver still follows you too closely, increase the distance between you and the vehicle ahead. This gives you and the tailgater more time to react in an emergency. Then, when the way is clear to pass safely, slow down so the tailgater can pass.

Sharing the road with large vehicles

It is very important to know how to safely share the road with large vehicles such as tractor-trailers and buses. Keep the following factors in mind:

- **Blind spots**

  Large vehicles have large blind spots on both sides. Avoid following too closely behind a large vehicle. Not only does it block your vision, but the driver of the large vehicle will not be able to see you back there. If the vehicle has to stop suddenly, you might crash into it. Remember that, if you can't see the driver's face in his or her side-view mirror, the driver probably can't see you.

- **Stopping distance**

  Many drivers do not realize that large vehicles require a much longer distance to stop than smaller vehicles. When passing a large vehicle, do not cut in front too closely. Not only is it discourteous, it is dangerous because it reduces the space cushion the large vehicle needs in order to stop safely if the need arises. When you are passing a large vehicle, make allowances for this longer stopping distance.

- **Wide turns**

  When making a right turn, a large vehicle may need to first swing wide to the left and then back around to the right in order to avoid hitting the right curb. If a large vehicle in front of you is making a right turn, do not move up into the space that opens up in the right lane; you are putting yourself into a very dangerous position. Once the front of the large vehicle has cleared the corner, the rest will move partially back into the right lane. If you are in that lane, your vehicle will be squeezed between the large vehicle and the curb. Instead, stay well back until the truck has completely cleared the lane. This situation can also occur on expressway off-ramps that have two left-turning lanes. Do not drive up into the left lane when a large vehicle is making a left turn in front of you. Stay well back until the truck has cleared the turn, or else you may get squeezed between the truck and the curb.

- **Rolling back**

  Leave plenty of room when you are stopped behind a large vehicle. When the driver of a large vehicle releases the brakes after being stopped, the large vehicle may roll back.

- **Spray**

  In bad weather, large vehicles are capable of spraying up large amounts of mud, snow, and debris, which could hit your face shield and block your vision, or even worse, cause you to lose control of your vehicle. Stay well back from large vehicles in bad weather.

- **Turbulence**
  Passing a large vehicle on a motorcycle or moped is difficult and can be dangerous. Due to various factors such as air pressure and airflow, a large vehicle can create heavy turbulence that can seriously affect your ability to control your vehicle when you are passing the larger one. If you must pass a large vehicle, try to relax and work with the air turbulence. After you pass through the first blast of turbulent air coming off the back of the truck, you will feel a stream of air either pulling you toward the truck or pushing you away from it, depending on wind direction. Lean away from the truck if the wind is pulling you toward it, or lean toward the truck if you are being pushed away. More turbulence will be waiting for you coming off the front of the truck. Lean into this wind as you pass in front of the truck.

A   Mid-block indented bays
B   An indentation before an intersection
C   An indentation after an intersection
D   Bus stops between legally parked cars

Sharing the road with municipal buses

Many municipal roadways have special indented stopping areas for municipal buses, called bus bays, where passengers can get on and off in safety.

There are three types of bus bays:
- Mid-block indented bay
- Indentations immediately before and after intersections
- Bus-stop areas between two designated parking areas

When a bus in a bus bay begins flashing its left-turn signals, indicating that it is ready to leave the bus bay, and you are approaching in the lane adjacent to the bus bay, you must allow the bus to re-enter traffic. Yielding the right-of-way to buses in this situation is the law.

IV. POSITIONING

Lane position

On a motorcycle or moped, you do not have the protection of a vehicle around you, so you have to make your own protection. To do this, you need to position your vehicle in the best possible spot on the road.

Depending on traffic and road conditions, the best position in the lane is usually a little to the left or right of the centre of the lane, in the track where the tires of a four-wheeled vehicle would travel. This spot is referred to as the left or right "tire track." It is considered the best position for keeping a safe distance from other vehicles, for seeing and being seen, and for the smoothest road surface with the best traction. It is also called the "blocking position" because it blocks or discourages other drivers from trying to squeeze past you in the same lane.

Limited-speed motorcycles and mopeds

If your vehicle is capable of maintaining the posted speed limit of the road, you should use the proper tire track position. However, if your vehicle cannot maintain the posted speed limit, you may drive as close as safely possible to the right-hand curb or edge of the roadway. You must allow faster vehicles to pass you when it is safe and practical to do so. Where it is dangerous to drive too close to the curb or edge of the roadway due to grates or other hazards, or if the lane is too narrow to safely allow vehicles to pass you, you may use a blocking position in the lane so that no one can pass you.

Wrong position
The centre of the lane is not a good driving position because it is coated with oil from other vehicles and gets slippery when wet.

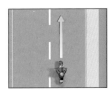

Curb lane
In the right lane of a two-lane road, you should be slightly to the left of the centre of the lane in the left tire track. This position provides good visibility and blocks other vehicles from pulling up beside you in the lane.

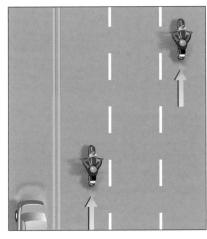

Passing lane
In the passing lane, you should be slightly to the right of the centre of the lane in the right tire track. This provides good visibility and blocks other vehicles from driving beside you in the lane.

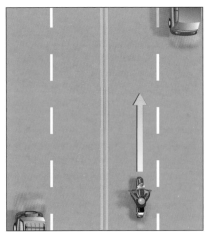

Centre lane
On a freeway with three or more lanes, do not drive in the centre lane, if possible, because you do not have a blocking position.

Right turn - same-size lane

Approaching an intersection where the curb lane remains the same size, stay in the normal blocking position (left tire track). Some motorcycle drivers angle their motorcycles across the lane (45 degrees) to create a larger blocking position and to make themselves more visible to drivers behind them. Make your turn and move to the correct lane position after completing the turn.

Right turn - wider lane

Making a right turn is more complicated when approaching an intersection where the lane opens up. Because the stop line is farther out, you must move over from your normal blocking position (left tire track) to prevent another vehicle from coming up on the inside on the wider part of the road. Check over your shoulder and move over to the right tire track. Again, you may want to angle your vehicle across the lane to make yourself more visible and to keep other vehicles from pulling up beside you. Make your right turn and then make another shoulder check if necessary

and move back to the proper blocking position (left tire track).

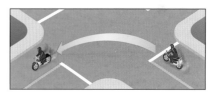

Left turn - from curb lane to curb lane

From the curb lane, make your turn, keeping your blocking position (left tire track) throughout the turn.

Left turn - from passing lane to passing lane

From the passing lane, make your turn, keeping your blocking position (right tire track) throughout the turn.

Changing lanes

Weaving in and out of heavy traffic is dangerous and is usually done by inexperienced or aggressive drivers. When you are travelling in heavy traffic, stay in the same lane as much as possible.

When you have to change lanes, check your mirrors to make sure there is no traffic overtaking you. If it is safe, signal, check your mirror again and then turn your head and check over your shoulder before changing lanes. Checking over your shoulder is the only sure way to see a vehicle behind you in the next lane. This is particularly important, because there is little chance a driver in the next lane can react quickly enough to avoid you once you have started to change lanes.

On a road with several lanes, check the far lanes as well as the one next to you. Another driver may be headed for the same space you are.

Lane sharing

Unless your vehicle cannot maintain the posted speed limit of the road and you are driving close to right curb or edge of the roadway, you should not share your lane with other vehicles. The best way to avoid lane sharing is to keep your blocking position, especially in situations where other drivers might be tempted to squeeze by you. This is most likely to happen in the following situations:
- Heavy bumper-to-bumper traffic
- When you are preparing to turn at an intersection
- When you are entering an exit lane or leaving the freeway
- When another driver wants to pass you.

Lane splitting

In heavy traffic, some motorcycle and moped drivers try "lane splitting" by driving on the line between lanes of traffic. This is extremely dangerous. Do not do it. It puts you too close to other vehicles. Other drivers do not expect a vehicle to be in that space. Just a small movement, such as a vehicle starting to change lanes or a door opening, can cause a collision because there is no place else for you to go.

Passing on the shoulder

The only time you may drive on the right shoulder of the road is to pass a vehicle turning left, and then only if the shoulder is paved. You may not pass on the left shoulder, whether it is paved or not.

Chapter 4, Section IV - Summary

By the end of this section, you should know:

- The concept of using tire track/block position to drive in the safest possible position on the road
- Various scenarios when you would use different lane positioning
- Which lane position you should use in various turns
- The danger of lane sharing, lane splitting and passing on the shoulder

CHAPTER 5
DEALING WITH PARTICULAR SITUATIONS

This chapter tells you how to deal with particular driving situations you will encounter. This includes freeway driving, driving at night and in bad weather. It gives you tips for driving on dangerous and difficult surfaces, driving in a group and carrying passengers or cargo.

Starting on a hill when driving a motorcycle with clutch and gears

Starting a motorcycle with a clutch and gears on a hill is more difficult than on level ground. Follow these steps to avoid stalling or rolling backward:

1. Use the front brake to hold the motorcycle while you start the engine and shift into first gear.
2. Change to the foot brake to hold the motorcycle while you operate the throttle with your right hand.
3. Twist the throttle a little bit for more power.
4. Release the clutch gradually. If you release it too quickly, the front wheel may lift off the ground or the engine may stall, or both.
5. Release the foot brake when the clutch begins to engage.

Vehicles turning left in front of you

One of the most common causes of collisions between motorcycles or mopeds and cars is the car driver turning left in front of the motorcycle or moped. This is because the car's driver either does not see the motorcycle or moped or misjudges its speed. You can help to avoid such collisions by following these steps:

• Prepare to slow down and proceed with caution if you are going faster than a driver would expect when you approach an intersection with a vehicle waiting to turn left.

• Take a defensive lane position. Move as far as possible to the right to give a little more room between you and the vehicle.

• Think about what you will do if the car turns in front of you. Where will you go? Is there a clear area to swerve? How fast will your motorcycle stop on the road surface?

• Do not focus only on the left-turning vehicle. Pay attention to everything going on around you. Check to make sure there is nothing else in the intersection that could cause trouble, such as another vehicle or a pedestrian.

Freeway driving (excludes LSMs and mopeds)

Note: The following sections deal with the freeway driving portion of the Level Two road test. If you take the road test on a limited-speed motorcycle or a moped, you will not do the freeway portion, since these vehicles are not allowed on freeways in Ontario. However, you should be familiar with the information contained in the following sections, as it may appear on the Level One knowledge test.

As a motorcyclist, you have to be careful not to drive too fast on a freeway. Although it is easy for motorcycles to cut through traffic and speed on a freeway, driving faster than traffic is dangerous because you will not be able to react quickly enough in an emergency.

Drive at a steady speed on a freeway. Keep checking traffic all around you and look in your mirrors every five to 10 seconds. As in city driving, you should be constantly scanning the road ahead and to each side, and checking your rearview mirrors. Look ahead to where you are going to be in the next 15 to 20 seconds, or as far ahead as you can see.

Always keep at least a two- to three-second distance behind the vehicle in front of you. If another vehicle follows too closely, give yourself even more room in front or change lanes. Keep a cushion of space all around you and avoid driving in the blind spots of other vehicles. Stay clear of large vehicles. They block your view more than other vehicles and create a strong air disturbance behind them. If you get behind one of these vehicles, the wall of wind can whip around your motorcycle, making it difficult to control.

Entering a freeway (excludes LSMs and mopeds)

Entrance ramps can be especially difficult for motorcycles. In addition to tight turns, entrance ramps often have slippery surfaces, causing you to drive more slowly than you would in a larger vehicle. And because other drivers are usually unaware of the risks faced by motorcyclists, you may have to deal with other vehicles tailgating or trying to pass you.

As you move along the ramp, check traffic in the lane you will move into and find a safe space to enter. Remember to look ahead and check your mirrors and your blind spots. Turn on your signal as soon as traffic on the freeway can see your motorcycle on the ramp. Increase your speed to match that of freeway traffic. Continue to divide your attention between watching in front, checking your mirrors and looking over your shoulder until you can merge safely with traffic. Merge in a smooth, gradual movement to the left tire track of the nearest freeway lane.

Changing lanes on a freeway (excludes LSMs and mopeds)

Be extra cautious when changing lanes on a freeway. On multi-lane roads you need to check that the lane is clear before you enter it, and you also need to make sure someone from another lane is not moving into that spot.

Because traffic moves so quickly on a freeway, it is especially important that you let vehicles behind you know that you intend to change lanes. Once you have made certain that a lane is clear, signal early and increase your speed slightly as you move into the lane. Watch to make sure that any vehicle behind you does not speed up.

When approaching an entrance ramp where other vehicles are merging onto the freeway, adjust your speed to allow the vehicle to merge safely ahead of you or behind you. This will help you avoid being hit by drivers who do not see you. If necessary, move over one lane and resume the curb lane when it is safe to do so.

Do the same thing when approaching exit ramps. If you are driving in the lane closest to the exit ramp, you may be cut off by a driver who does not see you and cuts across the lane in front of you to get to the exit ramp.

Leaving a freeway (excludes LSMs and mopeds)

When leaving a freeway, get into the right lane well before the exit and signal that you want to move into the exit lane, but do not slow down. Look left and right and check your mirrors. Turn on your signal. Enter the exit lane with a smooth, gradual motion. Once you are in the exit lane, reduce your speed gradually to the speed shown for the exit ramp. Check your speedometer to make sure you are going slowly enough. You may not realize how fast you are going because you are used to the high speed of the freeway.

If you miss an exit, keep going and take the next exit.

Driving on dangerous surfaces

Because motorcycles and mopeds balance on only two wheels, those two wheels must have good traction in order to stay upright. Any surface that affects your motorcycle or moped's traction will affect the steering, braking and balance. Slippery surfaces reduce your control and increase your chances of falling. It is almost impossible to keep your motorcycle or moped balanced on wet wooden surfaces or ice. If you cannot avoid such surfaces, slow down as much as possible before you get there.

Do not brake once on the slippery surface. If you are riding a motorcycle with a clutch and gears, pull in the clutch and coast across.

Pulling in the clutch removes the engine drag from the rear wheel and helps avoid skidding. Stay off the brakes. If necessary, use your foot to hold the motorcycle up.

Watch for uneven road surfaces such as bumps, broken pavement, potholes, railroad tracks and construction areas. If the condition of the road is bad enough, it could affect your control of your vehicle. Here are some tips on handling uneven surfaces:

• Slow down to reduce the impact.
• Keep your motorcycle or moped as upright as possible and avoid turning.
• Rise slightly on the footrests so that you can absorb the shock with your knees and elbows.

Traction on gravel roads is not as good as on pavement. Some areas are better than others. Stay in the tire tracks away from the loose gravel at the edge of the road.

Drive with extra care in a construction area. Slow down; the road could have ruts, mud or damaged pavement.

Stopping at railway crossings

All railway crossings on public roads in Ontario are marked with large red and white "X" signs. Watch for these signs and be prepared to stop. You may also see yellow advance warning signs and large "X" pavement markings ahead of railway crossings. Some railway crossings have flashing signal lights and some use gates or barriers to keep drivers from crossing the tracks when a train is coming. Some less-travelled crossings have stop signs posted.

On private roads, railway crossings may not be marked, so watch carefully. When you come to a railway crossing, remember the following:

- Slow down, listen and look both ways to make sure the way is clear before crossing the tracks.
- It can take up to two kilometres for a train to stop under full emergency braking.
- If a train is coming, stop at least five metres from the nearest rail or gate. Do not cross the track until you are sure the train or trains have passed.
- Never race a train to a crossing.
- If there are signal lights, wait until they stop flashing and, if the crossing has a gate or barrier, wait until it rises before you cross the tracks.
- Never drive around, under or through a railway gate or barrier while it is down, being lowered or being raised. It is illegal and dangerous.

- Avoid stopping in the middle of railway tracks. Make sure you have enough room to cross the tracks completely before you begin to cross.
- Avoid shifting gears while crossing tracks.
- If you get trapped on a crossing, immediately leave your vehicle and move to a safe place, then contact authorities.
- Buses and other public vehicles are required to stop at railway crossings that are not protected by gates, signal lights or a stop sign. School buses must stop at railway crossings whether or not they are protected by gates or signal lights. Watch for these vehicles, and be prepared to stop behind them.
- If you are approaching a railway crossing with a stop sign, you must stop unless otherwise directed by a flagman.

It is usually not necessary to change your path when crossing railway tracks that run across (perpendicular to) the road. Be prepared for a bump and avoid braking or turning while on the tracks. Railway and streetcar tracks are extremely slippery.

When you want to cross railroad or streetcar tracks that run parallel to your path, cross at a distinct angle (no less than 45 degrees) to prevent getting stuck in the tracks or losing control. Do not try to edge across the tracks or brake heavily. Do the same thing when crossing other uneven surfaces such as a pavement seams or a gravel shoulder.

Grooves, gratings and scraped roads

When you drive over certain surfaces, such as grooved or rutted pavement or metal bridge gratings, you may feel as though you are losing control of your motorcycle or moped. This effect is greater on smaller vehicles than it is on larger ones; the smaller your vehicle, the larger the effect. Avoid overreacting. Keep a gentle but firm grip on the handlebars and drive as smoothly as you can, choosing the best route possible until you get back on a good surface.

Driving at night

Driving a motorcycle or moped at night can be risky. You cannot see or be seen as well as you can in the daytime. Because of their inexperience, Level One (M1) drivers are not allowed to drive at night.

Another major problem for motorcycle and moped drivers when driving at night is alcohol. There are more drinking drivers on the road to put you at risk. And some motorcycle and moped drivers put themselves at risk by drinking. Alcohol reduces your ability to control your vehicle

and to anticipate trouble from other drivers. Follow these tips for driving at night:
- Keep your headlight(s) clean, and switch to your high beam whenever you are not following or approaching another vehicle. Get as much light as you can.
- Wear reflective clothing, such as a reflective vest and helmet. Also, wear warmer clothing when riding at night.

- Reduce your speed, particularly on roads that you do not know well. If there is something lying on the road ahead, you may not see it in time to avoid it.
- Use the lights of the vehicle in front of you to get a better view of the road ahead. Watch the movement of the vehicle's tail lights as well. Tail lights bouncing up and down can alert you to bumps or rough pavement.
- Increase your distance from other vehicles. You cannot judge distance as well at night. Make up for this by allowing extra distance between you and other vehicles. Give yourself more distance to pass.

Overdriving your headlight(s)

You are overdriving your headlight(s) when you go so fast that your stopping distance is farther than you can see with your headlight. This is a dangerous thing to do, because you are not giving yourself enough room to make a safe stop. Reflective road signs can mislead you as well, making you believe you can see farther ahead than you actually can. This may cause you to overdrive your headlight if you are not careful.

Driving in rain

Driving in rain can be risky. You are more likely to be tired and cold. The road is slippery, traction may be poor, visibility is reduced and your brakes may be less effective. The best thing to do is to sit it out. However, if you cannot avoid driving in the rain, here are some tips:

- **Make yourself visible.** Wear bright colours and reflective or fluorescent material.
- **Have good equipment.** Make sure you have good tire tread, a quality helmet and face shield, as well as warm clothing. A one-piece rain suit will help keep you warm and dry.

- **Reduce speed.** It takes a lot longer to stop on slippery surfaces. You must make up for this by driving at slower speeds. It is particularly important to reduce your speed on curves. Remember that speeds posted on curves apply to good surface conditions.
- **Avoid sudden moves.** Any sudden change in speed or direction can cause a skid on slippery surfaces. Turn, brake, accelerate and change gears as smoothly as possible.

- **Use both brakes.** Both brakes together are more effective than the back brake alone, even on a slippery surface.
- **Avoid the most slippery areas.** Oil from other vehicles tends to build up in the centre of the lane, particularly near intersections where vehicles slow down or stop. Avoid standing water, mud and other dangerous surfaces, such as wet metal or leaves.
- **Watch out for shiny areas and puddles.** Old worn pavement is often polished smooth and is very slippery when wet. You can spot these extra slippery sections if you look for shiny areas on the road surface. Puddles can hide potholes and traction is worse in deep water.
- **Avoid driving in puddles.** A puddle can hide a large pothole that could damage your vehicle or its suspension, or flatten a tire. The spray of water could obstruct the vision of adjacent motorists and result in

a collision, cause harm to nearby pedestrians or drown your engine, causing it to stall. Water can also make your brakes less effective.

• **Stay away from the edge of the road when you make sharp turns at intersections or enter or exit freeways.** Dirt and gravel tend to collect along the sides of the pavement and can cause you to slide.

Driving in fog

Fog is a thin layer of cloud resting on the ground. Fog reduces visibility for drivers, resulting in difficult driving conditions. The best thing to do is to avoid driving in fog. Check weather forecasts and, if there is a fog warning, delay your trip until it clears. It could save your life. If that is not possible or you get caught driving in fog, there are a number of safe driving tips you should follow on page 70.

Driving in cold weather

In winter or cold weather, other drivers do not expect to see motorcycles or mopeds out on the roads, even when road conditions are good. You must be even more careful and drive more defensively.

You need to anticipate sudden changes in the road surface, especially if the temperature is close to or below freezing. A road may be dry in one area, but wet and slippery in another. Watch for icy or snow-covered patches, which may appear on bridges, shady spots on the road, windswept areas and side roads that have not been completely cleared.

Be alert. Generally, asphalt is a grey-white colour in the winter. Be suspicious of black and shiny asphalt. The road may be covered with a thin layer of ice known as black ice.

It is best to avoid driving your motorcycle or moped when you know there is likely to be snow or ice. If you cannot avoid driving on a very slippery surface, slow down as much as possible before you get to it. If your motorcycle has a clutch and gears, pull in the clutch, coast across and stay off the brakes. If necessary, use your foot to hold your motorcycle or moped up. On a long section of snow-covered road, try to drive on loose or fresh snow. Hard-packed snow has less traction than loose snow.

The other danger of driving in winter is the cold. Cold affects your performance and that of your motorcycle or moped. Here are some things to watch for:
• Cold weather lowers tire pressure. Check it regularly.
• Face-shield fogging will be worse in cold weather.
• Probably your greatest danger is from fatigue brought on by the cold. Dress in multiple layers. Keep dry. Do not expose bare skin, and be alert to your own slowed reactions.

TIPS FOR DRIVING SAFELY IN FOG

Before you drive — and during your trip — check weather forecasts. If there is a fog warning, delay your trip until it clears. It could save your life. The best thing to do is to avoid driving in fog. If you are caught driving in fog, follow these safe driving tips:

DO:
- Pay full attention to your driving.
- Slow down gradually and drive at a speed that suits the conditions.
- Use your low-beam lights. The high beam reflects off the moisture droplets in the fog, making it harder to see.
- If you have fog lights on your vehicle, use them, in addition to your low beams.
- Be patient. Avoid passing, changing lanes and crossing traffic.

- Use pavement markings to help guide you. Use the right edge of the road as a guide, rather than the centre line.
- Increase your following distance. You will need extra distance to brake safely.
- Look and listen for any hazards that may be ahead.
- Watch for any electronically operated warning signs.
- Keep looking as far ahead as possible.
- Keep your windows and mirrors clean. Use your defroster and wipers to maximize your vision.
- If the fog is too dense to continue, pull completely off the road and try to position your vehicle in a safe parking area. Turn on your emergency flashers, in addition to keeping on your low-beam headlights.

DON'T:
- Don't stop on the travelled portion of the road. You could be hit from behind.
- Don't speed up suddenly, even if the fog seems to be clearing. You could find yourself suddenly back in fog.
- Don't speed up to pass a vehicle moving slowly or to get away from a vehicle that is following too closely.

REMEMBER:
- Watch your speed. You may be going faster than you think. If so, reduce speed gradually.
- Leave a safe braking distance between you and the vehicle ahead.
- When visibility is reduced, use your low-beam lights.
- Remain calm and patient. Don't pass other vehicles or speed up suddenly.
- Don't stop on the road. If visibility is decreasing rapidly, pull off the road into a safe parking area and wait for the fog to lift.

Driving in a group

If you want to drive with other motorcycle or moped drivers, you must do it in a way that is not dangerous and does not interfere with the flow of traffic.

Never drive directly alongside another motorcycle or moped. If you have to avoid another vehicle or something in the road, you will have no place to go. To speak to another driver, wait until you both have stopped.

The best way for a group of motorcycles or mopeds to drive together is in a "staggered formation." This means the leader drives on the left side of the lane while the second driver stays a little behind — about a one-second distance — and drives on the right side of the lane.

2 Seconds

2 Seconds

A third driver would take the left side, leaving a two-second distance behind the first driver. The fourth driver would be a two-second distance behind the second driver. This staggered formation allows the group to stay close together without reducing following distance and without having drivers drive alongside one another. Staggered formation can be safely used on an open road. However, you should drive in a single line on curves, in turns or when entering or leaving a freeway.

When drivers in a staggered formation want to pass another vehicle on the road, they should do it one at a time. When it is safe, the lead driver should pull out and pass. When the leader returns to the lane, she or he should move to the left of the lane and keep going to open a gap for the next driver. As soon as the first driver has passed safely, the second driver should move to the left of the lane and watch for a safe chance to pass. After passing, this driver should return to the right of the lane and open up a gap for the next driver.

Here are some tips to help you keep your group together without interfering with traffic or endangering others:

• **Plan ahead.** If you are the leader, look ahead for changes. Give signals early so the word gets back in plenty of time. Start lane changes early enough to let everyone complete the change.

• **Put beginner drivers up front.** Place inexperienced drivers behind the leader where they can be watched by more experienced drivers.

• **Check the driver behind you.** Let the driver at the back set the pace. Use your mirrors to keep an eye on the driver behind you. If she or he falls behind, slow down. If everyone does this, the group will stay together.

Driving in a group of slower-moving vehicles

When driving in a group of vehicles that cannot maintain the posted speed of the road, do not travel in staggered formation. Ride in single file and, when necessary, as close as possible to the right-hand curb or edge of the roadway. The "two-second rule" gives a minimum following distance. If you are travelling in a very large group, break into several smaller groups in order to allow faster traffic to pass.

Carrying passengers

The following section is applicable only to drivers of motorcycles, since it is an offence under the *Highway Traffic Act* to carry passengers on mopeds.

It is illegal for Level One (M1) drivers to carry passengers. Even with a Level Two (M2) licence, you should avoid carrying passengers or large loads until you are an experienced driver.

Before carrying a passenger, make certain your motorcycle is equipped to carry passengers. Your motorcycle seat must be large enough to hold both you and your passenger without crowding. The motorcycle must also have footrests for your passenger. Without a firm footing, your passenger can fall off, and pull you off too. Your passenger must also wear an approved helmet and protective clothing.

Adjust the mirrors and headlight to the change in the motorcycle's angle due to the extra weight. Have the passenger sit on the seat while you make the adjustments. If you carry a passenger, it is a good idea to add additional air pressure to the tires (check your owner's manual). If the suspension units are adjustable, they should also be adjusted to carry the added weight.

When carrying a passenger on a motorcycle, remember that your motorcycle will respond more slowly because of the extra weight. It takes longer to speed up, slow down or make a turn; the heavier the passenger, the slower the response. To adjust for the added weight, you should do the following:
- Drive at a lower speed, particularly on corners, curves and bumps.
- Begin to slow down earlier than usual when you approach a stop.

- Allow a greater following distance and keep more distance between you and vehicles to either side. Look for larger gaps when you cross, enter or merge with traffic.

Instruct your passenger before you start to drive. Do not assume your passenger knows what to do, even if he or she is a motorcycle driver. Warn your passenger when you are about to start moving, stop quickly, turn sharply or drive over a bump. Provide complete instructions before you start. You should tell your passenger to:
- Get on the motorcycle after the engine has started.
- Sit as far forward as possible without crowding you.
- Hold tightly to your waist or hips.
- Keep both feet on the footrests at all times, even when the motorcycle is stopped.
- Lean with the motorcycle.
- Avoid unnecessary motions or talk.

Carrying cargo
Follow these guidelines for carrying cargo:
- **Keep the load light.** Motorcycles and mopeds are not designed to carry much cargo. If you are using a top box or tank bags, do not overload them.
- **Keep the load low.** Do not pile loads against a frame on the back of the seat. This will change the centre of gravity and disturb the balance of the motorcycle or moped.
- **Keep the load forward.** Place the load over or in front of the rear axle. Anything mounted behind the rear wheel can affect how the vehicle turns and brakes. It can also cause wobble.
- **Distribute the load evenly.** If you have saddlebags, make certain the load in each is about the same. An uneven load can cause the vehicle to pull to one side.

- **Secure the load.** Make sure the load is securely fastened and near the centre of gravity. It is generally not a good idea to tie bundles to the top of the seat
- **Check the load.** Check the load regularly when you are stopped. Make sure it has not moved or become loose.

I. WHAT YOU NEED TO TOW A TRAILER IN ONTARIO

Towing a trailer behind a motorcycle

This section tells you what you need to know to tow a trailer in Ontario. This includes licence and registration requirements, as well as safety tips to follow when towing a trailer.

Before you attempt to tow a trailer, consider the size, power and condition of your vehicle. Make sure it is capable of towing both the trailer and the load you intend to carry, and that your trailer and hitch meet all the requirements described in this chapter.

Trailers that are towed behind motorcycles tend to be small and specially constructed, but must still comply with all the regulations of the *Ontario Highway Traffic Act*.

Note: Limited-speed motorcycles and mopeds are not suitable for towing trailers because of their smaller engine size.

Licence and permit

You must have a valid motorcycle licence (Class M1, M2(M), M2(L), M2, M(M), M(L) or M) to tow a trailer in Ontario.

Unless you are driving a commercial vehicle, it is against the law to tow more than one trailer behind your vehicle.

Registering your trailer

A trailer is considered a separate vehicle. Before you can tow one on any public road, you must register it and pay a one-time registration fee at a ServiceOntario centre. When you register your trailer, you will receive a licence plate and vehicle permit. Attach the licence plate to the back of your trailer where it is clearly visible. Always carry your permit, or a copy of it, to show to a police officer when asked for it.

Make sure your trailer is in good condition

Your trailer must be in safe operating condition. If it is not, a police officer may remove your trailer from the road until it is made safe to operate.

Lights

Your trailer must have:
- White licence plate light
- Red tail light
- Two red reflectors at the rear of the trailer, as far apart as possible

Your trailer must have mudguards, fenders and flaps, or be designed in such a way that it does not spray or splash traffic travelling behind you. You must always ensure that you have a clear view to the rear in your mirrors. The trailer must not obstruct this view.

Attaching your trailer

Your trailer must have two separate ways of attaching to your vehicle so that if one fails or comes loose, the trailer will stay attached.

No passengers

You may not carry any person in a trailer while it is being towed.

Trailer hitch

Use a good-quality trailer hitch. It should be securely attached to your vehicle, following the manufacturer's recommendations. The hitch ball should be installed so that, when the trailer is attached and tightened, it is level with no tilting.

In addition to a ball and hitch, you must use safety chains or cables, strong enough to hold the trailer and load, in case the ball and hitch accidentally come apart.

II. SAFE AND RESPONSIBLE TOWING

Loading your trailer

When loading your trailer, strap everything down both on the inside and outside of the trailer. Do not overload your trailer. Too much weight in the trailer can put a strain on the wheel bearings and axle, and make driving your motorcycle more difficult.

The distribution of the weight in your trailer is also very important. Generally, more of the trailer load should be in front of the trailer axle than behind it for proper hitch weight. About five to 10 per cent of the trailer's total weight should be supported on the hitch, within the weight limit marked on the hitch. Poor load balance can cause your trailer to sway or fishtail. The ball and hitch may also become separated, especially if there is too much weight in the rear of the trailer.

Starting out

Before each trip, check the trailer hitch, wheels, tires, lights, load distribution and load security to make sure they are safe. Check your tire pressure with the trailer loaded while the tires are still cold. When you start to drive, accelerate carefully. Drive slowly and carefully.

Curves and turns

If you are towing a trailer behind your motorcycle, you may need to adjust your position in the lane, compensating for the length and width of the trailer, in order to take a curve or turn. This positioning will vary on the size of the trailer being towed. When making any turn, always signal and check your mirrors and blind spots to make sure it is safe to turn.

Slowing down and stopping

A sudden stop can cause your trailer to jackknife or slide sideways or the load to shift. To avoid sudden stops, increase the following distance between you and the vehicle ahead. Keep out of the fast lanes and maintain a speed that will allow you to slow down and stop smoothly in any situation.

Passing

You cannot accelerate as quickly when you are towing a trailer. You also need more space because the length of your vehicle is much longer with a trailer attached. Before you pass, make sure you have enough time and room to complete the pass. Once you have passed, allow more room before you move back to your lane. Do not cut back into the lane too soon. This can cause your trailer to sway and make it difficult to control.

Being passed

If you are holding up a line of traffic, signal, pull over and let the other vehicles pass. Fast-moving trucks and buses create a strong air disturbance behind them. If a large bus or truck passes you, the wall of wind behind it may whip your trailer to the side, pushing it out of control. When you experience this, do not brake. Carefully steer your vehicle and trailer back into position. A slight increase in speed may help.

Chapter 5 - Summary

By the end of this section, you should know:
- How to deal with potentially difficult/dangerous situations like starting on a hill, vehicles turning left in front of you and crossing railway tracks
- Special considerations you must make when operating your motorcycle on a freeway
- How to deal with specific road and weather conditions
- The proper way for motorcyclists to drive in a group and how to safely carry passengers and cargo
- The requirements for properly and safely towing a trailer behind your motorcycle

CHAPTER 6
DEALING WITH EMERGENCIES

This chapter tells you how to be ready to deal with emergencies that may arise. Studies show that unprepared drivers too often freeze up or do the wrong thing when faced with an emergency.

Emergency braking

Review the section, "Braking," in chapter 3 of this handbook. Practice emergency stops in a safe environment, such as a vacant parking lot, to get a feel for it. The front brake supplies about three-quarters of your braking power, so use both brakes to stop quickly.

If your motorcycle is equipped with a clutch and gears, pull in the clutch and apply both brakes quickly and smoothly without locking the wheels. If either wheel locks, release the brake momentarily to get the wheel rolling, then re-apply the brakes but not to the point of locking. This is called threshold braking.

If your motorcycle or moped has an anti-lock braking system, practise emergency braking to understand how your vehicle will react. It is a good idea to practise doing this under controlled conditions with a qualified motorcycle instructor.

Anti-lock braking systems, which are also called ABS, are designed to sense the speed of the wheels on a vehicle. An abnormal drop in wheel speed, which indicates potential wheel lock, causes the brake force to be reduced to that wheel. This is how ABS prevents tire skid and the accompanying loss of steering control. This improves vehicle safety during heavy brake use or when braking with poor traction.

Although anti-lock braking systems help to prevent wheel lock, you should not expect the stopping distance for your motorcycle to be shortened. Under normal driving conditions on clean dry roads, you will notice no difference between braking with anti-lock brakes and braking without them.

If you are unfamiliar with ABS, the vibration that happens when you use them to brake hard in an emergency may surprise you. Make sure you know what to expect so you can react quickly and effectively in an emergency.

Emergency steering
Even a quick stop may not be enough to keep you from hitting something in your path. A vehicle ahead may stop suddenly or pull out and partly block the lane. The only way to avoid a collision may be to make a quick turn or swerve. The key to making a quick swerve is to get the motorcycle or moped to lean quickly in the direction you want to turn. It takes practice to do this smoothly and with confidence.

Taking a turn too fast
A major cause of motorcycle and moped collisions is running off the road in a turn or curve. One of two things seems to happen: either the driver badly misjudges a safe speed and takes the turn too fast, sliding off the road and crashing into something; or an inexperienced driver thinks he or she cannot turn sharply enough and brakes too hard, locking the wheels and sliding off the road and crashing. Inexperienced drivers sometimes crash at speeds at which a more experienced driver could manage the turn.

Until you learn the cornering limits of your vehicle, slow down for turns. Remember to brake before you turn.

Driving over objects
Sometimes you have no choice but to drive over an object in your path. Debris on the road, such as a length of tailpipe, may be too close for you to steer around. Driving over objects is similar to driving over uneven surfaces. These three steps will help

you drive safely over most objects you may find on the road:

1. Hold the handgrips tightly so that you do not lose your grip when the front wheel hits the object.
2. Keep a straight course. This keeps the motorcycle or moped upright and reduces the chance of falling.
3. Rise slightly on the footrests. This allows your arms and legs to absorb the shock and helps keep you from being bounced off as the rear wheel hits the object.

It is a good idea to stop and check your tires and rims for damage after driving over an object.

Flying objects

From time to time, insects, cigarette butts thrown from other vehicles or stones kicked up by the tires of the vehicle ahead may hit you. If you are not wearing face protection, you could be hit in the eye or the face.

If you are wearing face protection, it could become smeared or cracked, making it difficult to see. Whatever happens, do not let it affect your control of your motorcycle or moped. Keep your eyes on the road and your hands on the handlebars. As soon as it is safe, pull off the road and repair the damage.

Animals on the road

You should do everything you can to avoid swerving around an animal on the road. Swerving is very dangerous as it may cause you to hit another vehicle. If you encounter an animal on the road, brake and prepare to stop. If you cannot stop in time and the animal is large, such as a dog or moose, you may have no choice but to swerve; if you are in traffic, try to remain in your lane. However, if the animal is small, you have a better chance of surviving an impact with it than with another vehicle.

Dogs often chase motorcycles and mopeds. If you find yourself being chased, do not kick at the animal. It is too easy to lose control of your vehicle.

What to do if a tire blows out

If you have a tire blowout, you need to react quickly to keep your balance. You cannot always hear a tire blow. You have to be able to detect a flat tire from the way the motorcycle reacts. If the front tire goes flat, the steering will feel heavy. If the rear tire goes flat, the back of the motorcycle or moped will tend to slide from side to side.

If you have a tire blowout while driving, take the following steps:

1. Hold the handgrips tightly and concentrate on steering. Try to keep a straight course.
2. Stay off the brake. Gradually close the throttle and let the vehicle coast.

3. If it is the front tire that has blown, shift your weight as far back as you can. If it is the rear tire, stay where you are.
4. Wait until you are going very slowly, then edge toward the side of the road and coast to a stop.

What to do if the throttle gets stuck (if applicable)

When you try to close the throttle you may find that it will not turn or the engine will not slow down. Here is what to do:
1. Relax and let up on the throttle.
2. At the same time, pull in the clutch and turn off the engine with the kill switch.
3. If the motorcycle does not have a kill switch, pull in the clutch and let the engine race until you can stop, and turn it off with the key. You may also be able to leave the clutch out and stop the engine with the brakes.

4. Park the motorcycle until you can get it fixed.

What to do in a wobble

When driving at a fairly high speed, the front wheel can suddenly begin to wobble or shake from side to side. The only thing you can do in a wobble is to drive it out as follows:
1. Firmly grip the handlebars. Do not try to fight the wobble.
2. Gradually close the throttle and let the vehicle slow down. Do not apply the brakes; it could make the wobble worse. Never accelerate.
3. Pull off the road as soon as you can stop.
4. If you are carrying a heavy load, distribute it more evenly. If you are at a gas station or have a tire gauge, check your tire pressure.

Other causes of wobbling

Other things that can cause a motorcycle or moped to wobble are:
• Windshield improperly mounted or not designed for your particular vehicle
• Loose steering-head bearings
• Worn steering parts
• Wheel that is bent out of alignment
• Loose wheel bearings
• Loose spokes
• Improper tire-tread design

What to do if a chain breaks

Chain failure usually is caused by a worn or stretched chain, which does not fit the sprockets properly, or by worn sprockets. You will notice if the chain breaks because you will instantly lose power to the rear wheels, and the engine will speed up. If the chain locks the rear wheel, you will not be able to disengage it, and it will cause your motorcycle to skid. Try to maintain control and find a safe place to pull off the road as soon as possible.

What to do if your engine seizes

Engine seizure means that the engine locks or freezes. It has the same result as a locked rear wheel. However, there is usually some advance warning of engine seizure, giving you time to respond.

Overheating or a lack of lubrication causes engine seizure. Without oil, the engine's moving parts will no longer move smoothly against each other, and the engine will overheat. The first symptom may be a loss of engine power. You may also notice a change in the engine's sound.

Pull off the road to the shoulder and stop. Let the engine cool. While you may be able to add oil and restart the engine, it should be thoroughly checked for damage.

If your motorcycle has a clutch and gears and the engine starts to seize, squeeze the clutch lever, disengaging the engine from the rear wheel, then pull off the road to stop.

Getting off the road

If you have to leave the road to check your vehicle or to rest for a while, check the surface of the roadside to make sure it is hard enough to drive on. If it is soft grass, loose sand or if you are not sure about it, slow right down before you turn onto it. Since drivers behind may not expect you to slow down, make sure to check your mirror and signal.

Pull as far off the road as you can. A motorcycle or moped by the side of the road can be very hard to spot. You do not want someone else pulling off at the same place.

If you need help, place your helmet on the ground near the road. This is a signal among motorcycle drivers that a motorcyclist needs help.

Chapter 6 - Summary

By the end of this chapter, you should know:

- How to deal with mechanical problems such as a blown tire, stuck throttle, wobble, broken chain or seized engine
- How to perform emergency braking and steering manoeuvres and how to avoid taking a turn too fast
- How to deal with objects or animals on the road or flying objects hitting you while you are driving
- How to safely pull over to the side of the road

CHAPTER 7
KEEPING YOUR MOTORCYCLE OR MOPED ON THE ROAD

This chapter tells you about the rules you must follow for registering and insuring your motorcycle and moped, and about buying and selling a used motorcycle or moped. It also tells you what to do to keep your motorcycle or moped running safely.

Insuring your motorcycle or moped
Ontario has compulsory motor-vehicle insurance. This means that you must insure your motorcycle or moped.

You must show proof that you have insurance coverage before you can register your motorcycle or moped, or renew your registration. If you do not tell the truth about your insurance, or show false documents, you can be fined $5,000 to $25,000. You may also lose your licence for up to one year and have your motorcycle or moped taken away for up to three months.

You must insure all your vehicles for third-party liability of at least $200,000. This covers you if you injure or kill someone, or damage someone's property. Collision insurance to cover damage to your own vehicle is a good idea but not required by law.

When driving your own vehicle or someone else's, you must carry the pink liability insurance card given to you by the insurance company for that particular vehicle. You must show this card when a police officer asks for it. If you do not, you can be fined up to $400.

Registering your motorcycle or moped

Motorcycle and moped registration includes licence plates and a vehicle permit. Licence plates are required for motorcycles and mopeds when driven on public roads.

When registering your moped at a ServiceOntario centre, you must show the bill of sale. Dealers of mopeds are required by law to provide purchasers with a certificate that guarantees the moped fits the definition under the *Highway Traffic Act*.

A distinct new licence plate is issued to all limited-speed motorcycles in the same size as the motorcycle plate but is green with white lettering. Motorcycle and moped plates will remain the same. Licence plates in Ontario work on a plate-to-owner system. This means that licence plates move with the vehicle owner, not the vehicle. When you sell or change a vehicle, you must remove the plates. If you do not intend to use them on another vehicle, you may return them to a ServiceOntario centre.

Keep your licence plate visible

By law, your entire licence plate must be **completely visible**. Remove anything that makes it difficult to see your licence plate, such as dirt, snow, a licence-plate frame or a bike.

If your licence plate is not visible, you may be fined.

Your vehicle permit must have an accurate description of your vehicle. This means if you change anything about your motorcycle or moped, such as the colour, you must report it to a ServiceOntario centre within six days. Also, if you change your name or address, you must notify the Ministry of Transportation within six days. You can do this in person at a ServiceOntario centre or by mailing the correct information stub attached to your vehicle permit to the Ministry of Transportation, P.O. Box 9200, Kingston, ON, K7L 5K4; or online at www.serviceontario.ca.

Buying or selling a used motorcycle or moped

If you are selling a used motorcycle privately in Ontario, you must buy a used-vehicle information package (UVIP). (You do not need one if you are selling a moped.) The package is available from any ServiceOntario centre and online at www.serviceontario.ca.

This package, which the seller must show to potential buyers, has a description of the motorcycle, its registration and lien history in Ontario, and the average wholesale and retail values for its model and year. It also includes information about retail sales tax. The seller gives the UVIP to the buyer.

Sellers of both motorcycles and mopeds must remove their licence plates, sign the vehicle transfer portion of the vehicle permit and give it to the buyer. Sellers must keep the plate portion of the permit.

The buyer must take the UVIP (except if buying a moped) and the vehicle portion of the permit to a Driver and Vehicle Licence Issuing Office to register as the new owner within six days of the sale.

Before buyers can put their own plates on their new vehicle, they must have:

- The licence plates validated, if not already valid
- The vehicle portion of the permit issued for that vehicle
- The licence plate number recorded on the plate portion of the vehicle permit
- Valid safety standards certificate (does not apply to mopeds)

Buying and Selling a Used Vehicle in Ontario

Ⓟ Ontario

- The minimum insurance required under the *Compulsory Automobile Insurance Act*

Safety Standards Certificate

A safety standards certificate is a document that certifies a vehicle's fitness. You can buy and register a vehicle without a safety certificate, but you cannot put your own plates on the vehicle or drive it without one.

An inspection station licensed by the Ministry of Transportation to inspect motorcycles can issue a safety standards certificate, provided your vehicle passes an inspection. Many garages are licensed — look for a sign saying it is a motor vehicle inspection station.

A safety standards certificate is valid for 36 days after the inspection However, the certificate is not a guarantee or warranty. Mopeds are exempt from the certificate requirement.

Maintaining your motorcycle or moped

Motorcycles and mopeds require more maintenance than cars. It is important that you read your owner's manual, inspect your motorcycle carefully and fix things right away. In addition to the check you do each time you drive (see chapter 2), here are some things you should examine each week:

- **Tires**

    Your tire tread should be at least 1.5 millimetres deep. If the tread is getting low, buy new tires. Inadequate tread depth will greatly reduce your braking traction on wet roads. If the wear is uneven, you need to find

out why it is happening and fix the problem. Also check for cuts, cracks, scrapes, exposed cord, abnormal bumps or bulges or any other visible tread or sidewall defect. Also check the air pressure regularly.

- **Wheels**

    Check both wheels for missing or loose spokes. Check the rims for cracks or dents. Lift the wheel off the ground and spin it, if possible. Watch its motion and listen for noise. Also, move it from side to side to check for looseness.

Coolant

If your engine is liquid-cooled, check the coolant level. At the same time, inspect the radiator hoses, looking for cracks and leaks.

Battery (if your vehicle is equipped with one)

Check your battery fluid level regularly.

Drive line

Clean and oil the chain and check it for wear. Replace it when necessary. Your owner's manual will describe when and how to adjust a chain. If your motorcycle has a shaft drive, check the fluid level.

Shock absorbers

If your motorcycle bounces several times after crossing a bump or you hear a clunk, your shock absorbers may need to be adjusted or replaced.

- ## Fastenings

  Check for loose or missing nuts, bolts or cotter pins. Keeping your motorcycle or moped clean makes it easier to spot missing parts.
- ## Brakes

  If you hear a scraping sound when you try to stop, or if the brakes feel spongy, have them serviced immediately. If your motorcycle has hydraulic brakes, check the fluid level regularly.

Accessories and modifications

Making changes or adding accessories incorrectly can make a motorcycle or moped dangerous to drive. Before adding accessories or modifying your motorcycle or moped, make certain that the alteration will not affect the safety and performance of your vehicles, and that the alteration complies with the requirements of the *Highway Traffic Act*. If you are not

sure, check with the manufacturer of your motorcycle or moped.

- ## Extended forks

  Some drivers install longer-than-standard forks for styling. However, they reduce steering precision and increase stress on the motorcycle or moped frame and steering components.
- ## Road race handlebars

  Extra-low clamp-on handlebars make it harder to do proper shoulder checks and may cause discomfort and fatigue.
- ## Touring modifications

  Improperly designed or installed fairings, luggage attachments and containers may overload the motorcycle, change its handling characteristics or cause a tire blowout.

CHOOSING A MOTORCYCLE SAFETY COURSE

Every new driver, or those wishing to improve their skills, should take a motorcycle training course. If you pass a ministry-approved motorcycle safety course, you can reduce the time you must spend at Level Two by four months. A course may also offer the following:

- Personal instruction from experts
- A motorcycle provided for about 14 hours of practice
- Your Level One or Level Two driving test
- Valuable tips and skills to keep you safe on the road
- The possibility of an insurance discount on your motorcycle (check with your insurance company)

If you would like more information about motorcycle or limited-speed motorcycle driver training or a course being held near you, call your local community college or visit the Ministry of Transportation website at www.mto.gov.ca.

Chapter 7 - Summary
By the end of this chapter, you should know:
- The mandatory insurance requirements for motorcycles
- Information regarding registering, buying or selling a used motorcycle and safety standards certificates
- Components of your motorcycle that should be checked weekly and what to look for
- That some modifications to your motorcycle are dangerous and illegal
- Some elements to consider when choosing a motorcycle safety course

CHAPTER 8
THE LEVEL ONE ROAD TEST

Statistics show that new drivers of any age are far more likely to be involved in serious or fatal collisions than experienced drivers.

To help new drivers develop better, safer driving habits, Ontario introduced graduated licensing in 1994 for all drivers applying for their first car or motorcycle licence. Graduated licensing lets you gain driving skills and experience gradually, in lower-risk environments. The two-step licensing system takes at least 20 months to complete and includes two road tests.

Passing the Level One (M1) road test allows you to move to Level Two and receive a Class M2 licence. If you have passed the test on a limited-speed motorcycle or a moped, an L condition is added to your driver's licence. The L condition means you are restricted to driving a limited-speed motorcycle or moped on only certain roads.

If you have passed the test on a three-wheeled motorcycle, an M condition is added to your driver's licence. The M condition means you are restricted to driving only three-wheeled motorcycles.

The Level One road test deals with basic driving skills. It includes a three-part motorcycle skill test. Sets of two cones placed one metre apart, with each set 4.5 metres apart (from the centre of the cone), are used to test your skill in manoeuvring your motorcycle.

Road tests are conducted according to set time frames. It is best to arrive early in order to complete the registration process and be ready for your test at the proper time. When you arrive, your examiner will tell you how long you have to complete the test.

The following details each part of the Level One test:

Walk test

Walk the motorcycle or moped around the cones in a figure eight, preferably with both hands on the handgrips. Without losing control or dropping the vehicle, stop the front wheel on the stop line at the end of the figure eight.

Serpentine drive

While moving slowly and keeping both feet on the footrests, drive in a serpentine pattern in a controlled manner.

Straight-line brake test

While moving slowly and keeping both feet on the footrests, drive in a straight line between the rows of cones. Turn and accelerate in preparation for the brake test. Bring the vehicle to a quick, safe, controlled stop using both brakes evenly with the front wheel on the finish line.

This test is to determine balance and control at low speeds and is meant to be done in one continual motion. If you must put a foot down or you knock a cone over, recover as best you can and continue on.

Note: All Drive Test Centres may not be able to accommodate Level One tests for motor tricycles. For more information, you should check the DriveTest website at www.drivetest.ca.

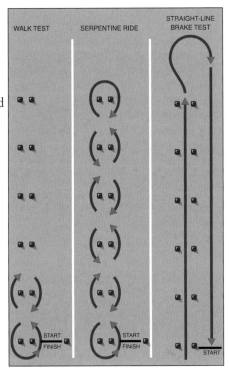

On-road driving demonstration

This illustration shows a typical on-road driving route used at DriveTest Centres across the province that give motorcycle tests.

Your examiner will watch your demonstration from a strategic location where the bike can be observed at several intersections. You are expected to obey all the rules of the road, signal all your intentions, maintain a good blocking position, keeping yourself visible to other traffic. You will be marked on your lane positioning, your turning arcs, your use of the vehicle's controls and your observation of traffic.

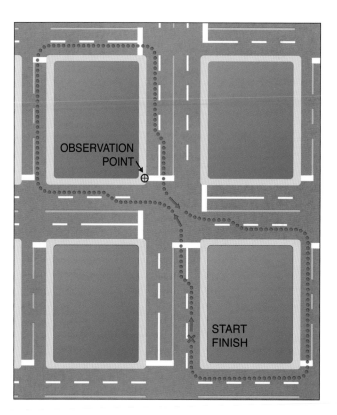

OBSERVATION POINT

START FINISH

CHAPTER 9
THE LEVEL TWO ROAD TEST

The Level Two road test deals with advanced knowledge and skills that are generally gained with driving experience.

When you take the test, the examiner will follow you in another vehicle and talk to you by radio through a disposable earphone. The examiner will give you directions. As you complete the driving tasks, the examiner will watch to make sure you successfully perform the actions associated with them.

To help prepare for the Level Two road test, this chapter tells you the various tasks and actions that you will be expected to perform.

Limited-speed motorcycles and mopeds

If your vehicle is capable of maintaining the posted speed limit of the road, you should use the proper tire-track position. However, if your vehicle cannot maintain the posted speed limit, you may drive as close as safely possible to the right-hand curb or edge of the roadway. You must allow faster vehicles to pass you when it is safe to do so. Where it is dangerous to drive too closely to the curb or edge of the roadway due to grates or other hazards, or if the lane is too narrow to safely allow vehicles to pass you, you may use a blocking position in the lane so that no one can pass you.

I. LEFT AND RIGHT TURNS

The approach

This driving task begins when the examiner tells you to make a left or right turn and ends at the point just before you enter the intersection. Make sure you take the following actions:

Traffic check

Before slowing down, look all around you. Use your mirrors to check traffic behind you, and check your blind spot. If you change lanes, remember to check your blind spot.

Lane

Move into the far left or far right lane as soon as the way is clear. If possible, change lanes before you begin to slow down for the turn. Generally, use the left tire track to turn left from a one-lane road and the right tire track to turn left from a two-lane road. A right turn is usually made from the left tire track of the far right lane.

Signal

Turn on your signal before slowing down for the turn unless there are vehicles waiting to enter the road from side roads or driveways between you and the intersection. Wait until you have passed these entrances so that drivers will not think you are turning before the intersection.

Speed

Steadily reduce speed as you approach the turn. If your motorcycle has a clutch and gears, downshift into a lower gear as you slow down, but do not rely on downshifting only to slow down. Use both your front and rear brakes. This will also let other drivers know that you are slowing down. Do not drive slower than the speed at which your vehicle is stable (about 15 km/h). At such low speed, the vehicle may weave to keep upright. Even if you are skilled enough to balance the motorcycle without weaving, the low speed leaves you with only minimum control.

Space

While slowing down, keep at least a two- to three-second distance behind the vehicle in front of you.

If stopped

You will need to do this driving task if you cannot complete your turn without stopping, either because the way is not clear or you face a stop sign or red traffic light. Remember to do the following:

1. With both front and rear brakes on, come to a complete stop.
2. At the point of stopping, put your left foot down while still keeping both brakes on. Do not put your foot down until you can do so without dragging it along the ground.
3. Once stopped, do not let your motorcycle or moped roll forward or backward.
4. Keep the brake light showing while stopped.
5. When traffic conditions allow, move forward to check that the way is clear or to start the turn.
6. If you have to stop after you have passed the stop line, do not back up.

Tire track

Stop in the correct tire track to block other vehicles from pulling up beside you in the lane. Generally, use the left tire track when turning left from a one-lane road and the right tire track when turning left from a two-lane road. A right turn is usually made from the left tire track of the far right lane. When you stop, you may point your motorcycle or moped in the direction of the turn to let other drivers know you are turning and to keep them from pulling up beside you. If you stop behind a large vehicle, make sure the driver can see you through a side mirror.

Space

When stopped behind another vehicle at an intersection, leave enough space to pull out and pass without having to back up — about one motorcycle length. If the vehicle in front is large, leave more space.

Leaving this space protects you in three ways: it lets you pull around the vehicle in front if it stalls; it helps prevent you from being pushed into the vehicle ahead of you if you are hit from behind; and it reduces the risk of collision if the vehicle ahead rolls backward or backs up.

Stop line

If you are the first vehicle approaching an intersection with a red light or stop sign, stop behind the stop line if it is marked on the pavement. If there is no stop line, stop at the crosswalk, marked or not. If there is no crosswalk, stop at the edge of the sidewalk. If there is no sidewalk, stop at the edge of the intersection.

Turning

This driving task involves your actions as you make the turn. Remember to do the following:

Traffic check

If you are stopped, waiting for a green light or for the way to be clear, keep checking traffic all around you. Just before entering the intersection, look left, ahead and right to check that the way is clear. If there is any doubt about the right-of-way, try to make eye contact with nearby drivers or pedestrians. If it is possible for another vehicle to overtake you while you are turning, check your blind spot before starting to turn. You have not properly checked traffic if another vehicle or pedestrian has the right-of-way and must take action to avoid your vehicle.

Both feet

Keep both feet on the footrests throughout the turn. Do not walk

the motorcycle or moped to ease into or around a turn. You are most at risk from other traffic when turning. Keeping both feet on the footrests gives you maximum control when you need it most.

Gears (if applicable)

Do not shift gears during the turn. An incorrect gear change during a turn can cause the rear wheel to skid. Generally, not changing gears gives you more control and balance over your vehicle when it is turning.

Speed

Move ahead within four to five seconds after it is safe to start. Increase speed enough that the engine does not stall or over-rev. Make the turn at a steady speed, slow enough to keep full control of the motorcycle or moped while turning, but fast enough to keep your balance and not slow down other traffic.

Wide/short

Turn into the corresponding lane on the intersecting road without going over any lane markings or curbs.

Completing the turn

This driving task completes the turn. It begins when you enter the intersecting road and ends when you return to normal traffic speed. Take the following actions:

Lane

End your turn in the lane that corresponds to the lane you turned from. Generally, you should end the turn in the left tire track. If you are turning left onto a multi-lane road, return to normal traffic speed and move into the curb lane when it is safe to do so. If you are turning right onto a road where the right lane is blocked with parked vehicles or cannot be used for other reasons, move directly to the next available lane.

Traffic check
As you return to normal traffic speed, check your mirrors to become aware of the traffic situation on the new road.

Speed
Return to normal traffic speed by accelerating smoothly to blend with the traffic around you. In light traffic, accelerate moderately. In heavier traffic, you may have to accelerate more quickly. If your vehicle is equipped with gears, shift gears as you increase speed.

Cancel signal
Turn off your signal if it does not work automatically.

II. STOP INTERSECTION

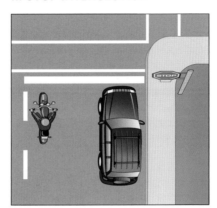

The approach
This driving task is done at intersections where you must come to a stop. It begins at the point where you can see the intersection and ends just before you enter the intersection. Be sure to follow these actions:

Traffic check
Before slowing down, look all around you. Check your mirrors and your blind spots.

Speed
Steadily reduce speed as you approach the intersection. Downshift into a lower gear as you slow down, but do not rely on downshifting only to slow down. Use both your front and rear brakes. This will also let other drivers know that you are slowing down. Do not drive slower than the speed at which your motorcycle or moped is stable (about 15 km/h). At such low speed, the motorcycle or moped may weave to keep upright. Even if you are skilled enough to balance the motorcycle without weaving, the low speed leaves you with only minimum control.

Space
While slowing down, keep at least a two- to three-second distance behind the vehicle in front of you.

The stop

This task includes the actions you take as you drive through the intersection and return to normal traffic speed. Be sure to follow these actions:

Stop

With both front and rear brakes on, come to a complete stop. At the point of stopping, put your left foot down while still keeping both brakes on. Do not put your foot down until you can do so without dragging it along the ground. Once stopped, do not let your motorcycle or moped roll forward or backward. Keep the brake light showing while stopped. When traffic conditions allow, move forward to check that the way is clear or to start across the intersection. If you have to stop after you have passed the stop line, do not back up.

Tire track

Stop in the correct tire track to block other vehicles from pulling up beside you in the lane. Generally, this will be the same one you used when approaching the intersection. However, if you stop behind a large vehicle, make sure the driver can see you through a side mirror.

Space

When stopped behind another vehicle at an intersection, leave enough space to pull out and pass without having to back up — about one motorcycle length. If the vehicle in front is a large vehicle, leave more space. Leaving this space protects you in three ways: it lets you pull around the vehicle in front if it stalls; it helps prevent you from being pushed into the vehicle ahead of you if you are hit from behind; and it reduces the risk of collision if the vehicle ahead rolls backward or backs up.

Stop line

If you are the first vehicle approaching an intersection with a red light or stop sign, stop behind the line if it is marked on the pavement. If there is no stop line, stop at the crosswalk, marked or not. If there is no crosswalk, stop at the edge of the sidewalk. If there is no sidewalk, stop at the edge of the intersection. Stop in a position where other vehicles cannot pull up beside you in the lane.

Driving through

This task includes the actions you take as you drive through the intersection and return to normal traffic speed. Be sure to follow these actions:

Traffic check

If you are stopped, waiting for a green light or the way to be clear, keep checking traffic all around you. Just before entering the intersection, look left, ahead and right to check that the way is clear. If there is any doubt about the right-of-way, try to make eye contact with nearby drivers or pedestrians. You have not properly checked traffic if another vehicle or pedestrian has the right-of-way and must take action to avoid your motorcycle.

Gears (if applicable)

Do not shift gears crossing the intersection. If you need to, you may shift gears immediately after your motorcycle is moving, but before it is well into the intersection. You may also shift gears in an intersection wider than four lanes, if not doing so would slow down other traffic. Generally, not changing gears gives you more control over your motorcycle.

Traffic check

As you return to normal traffic speed, check your mirrors to become aware of the traffic situation after you have gone through the intersection.

Speed

Move ahead within four to five seconds after it is safe to start. Return to normal traffic speed by accelerating smoothly to blend with the traffic around you. In light traffic, accelerate moderately. In heavier traffic, you may have to accelerate more quickly. If your vehicle is equipped with gears, shift gears as you increase speed.

III. THROUGH INTERSECTION

The approach

This driving task is done at intersections where you may not need to stop. It begins at the point where you can see the intersection and ends just before the entrance to the intersection. Remember to do the following:

Traffic check

As you approach the intersection, look left and right for traffic on the intersecting road. If you have to slow down for the intersection, check your mirrors for traffic behind you.

Speed

Keep at the same speed as you go through the intersection unless there is a chance traffic may cross the intersection in front of you. If so, slow down and be ready to stop. Watch for pedestrians about to cross the intersection and vehicles edging into the intersection or approaching at higher speeds. Steadily reduce speed as you approach the intersection. Downshift into a lower gear as you slow down, but do not rely on downshifting only to slow down. Use both your front and rear brakes. This will also let other drivers know that you are slowing down. Do not drive slower than the speed at which

your motorcycle or moped is stable (about 15 km/h). At such low speed, the motorcycle or moped may weave to keep upright. Even if you are skilled enough to balance the motorcycle or moped without weaving, the low speed leaves you with only minimum control.

Space

Keep at least a two- to three-second distance behind the vehicle in front of you.

Driving through

This driving task includes your actions from the time you enter the intersection until you have crossed it and are returning to normal traffic speed. Remember these points:

Lane

Do not go over lane markings or change tire tracks in the intersection. If a vehicle turning left or a vehicle edging into the intersection from the

right blocks your lane, slow down or stop instead of pulling out to go around the vehicle.

Gears (if applicable)

Do not shift gears crossing the intersection. If you need to, you may shift gears immediately after your motorcycle is moving but before it is well into the intersection. You may also shift gears in an intersection wider than four lanes if not doing so would slow down other traffic. Generally, not changing gears gives you more control over your motorcycle.

Traffic check

If you slowed down for the intersection, check your mirrors again before returning to normal traffic speed.

IV. FREEWAY

Entering
(This section does not apply when taking the test on a limited-speed motorcycle or moped.)

This driving task begins on the entrance ramp to a freeway and ends when you have reached the speed of traffic on the freeway. Remember to do the following:

Traffic check

While on the ramp, as soon as you can see freeway traffic approaching from behind, check your mirrors and your blind spot for a space to merge safely. At the same time, watch any vehicles in front of you on the ramp and keep back a safe distance. Continue to divide your attention between watching in front, checking your mirrors and looking over your shoulder to check your blind spot until you can merge safely with traffic.

Signal

If you have not done so already, turn on your signal as soon as traffic on the freeway is able to see your motorcycle on the ramp.

Space

Drive in the left tire track. While on the ramp and merging with freeway traffic, keep at least a two- to three-second distance behind the vehicle in front of you. If traffic is heavy or moving at such a high speed that it is difficult to keep an ideal following distance, change your speed to get the best spacing possible.

Speed

On the ramp, do not drive faster than the safe ramp speed. While in the acceleration lane, increase your speed to match that of freeway traffic. While merging, control your speed to blend smoothly with freeway traffic.

Merge

Merge with freeway traffic in a smooth, gradual movement to the left tire track of the nearest freeway lane.

Cancel Signal

Turn off your signal as soon as you have merged with freeway traffic.

Driving along
(This section does not apply when taking the test on a limited-speed motorcycle or moped.)

This driving task checks your actions driving along the freeway but not merging, changing lanes or exiting. Be sure to remember the following points:

Traffic check

While driving along, keep checking traffic all around you and look in your mirrors every five to 10 seconds.

Speed

Avoid exceeding the speed limit or driving unreasonably slowly. Drive at a steady speed whenever possible. Look ahead to where you are going to be in the next 12 to 15 seconds for dangerous situations or obstacles that you can avoid by changing your speed.

Space

Always keep at least a two- to three-second distance behind the vehicle in front of you. If another vehicle follows too closely behind you, give yourself even more room in front or change lanes. Try to keep a space on both sides of your motorcycle and avoid driving in the blind spots of other vehicles. Try not to drive behind large vehicles. Because of their size, they block your view of traffic more than other vehicles. Drive in the correct tire track.

Exiting
(This section does not apply when taking the test on a limited-speed motorcycle or moped.)

This driving task begins when you are driving in the far right lane of the freeway and can see the exit you want to take. It ends when you reach the end of the exit ramp. Remember to do the following:

Traffic check

Before moving into the exit lane, look left and right and check your mirrors. If there is a lane of traffic on your right, such as an acceleration lane from an entrance ramp, or a paved shoulder, remember also to check your right blind spot.

Signal

Turn on your signal before you reach the exit lane.

Exit lane

Enter the exit lane at the beginning of the lane with a smooth, gradual movement. Drive in the left tire track and stay inside the lane markings.

Speed

Do not slow down before you are completely in the exit lane. Once you are in the lane, gradually slow down without causing traffic to pile up behind you. Use both your front and rear brakes to slow down. This will let other drivers know that you are slowing down. Downshift as you reduce speed.

Space

Keep at least a two- to three-second distance behind the vehicle in front of you.

Cancel signal

Turn off your signal once you are on the exit ramp.

V. LANE CHANGE

This driving task begins as you look for a space to change lanes and ends when you have completed the lane change. Remember to follow these actions:

Traffic check

While waiting to change lanes safely, look all around you. Divide your attention between watching in front, watching the mirrors, and checking your blind spot. If there is another lane beside the one you are moving into, check traffic in that lane to avoid colliding with a vehicle moving into the lane at the same time as you.

Signal

Turn on your signal when there is enough space for you to change lanes. After signalling, check your blind spot one more time before starting to move into the other lane. Your signal should be on soon enough to give traffic behind you time to react to the signal. If traffic in the lane you are moving into is heavy, you may turn on your signal before there is enough space to change lanes. This will let traffic behind you know that you are looking for a space to change lanes.

Space

Keep at least a two- to three-second distance behind the vehicle in front of you. If there is another lane beside the one you are moving into, be careful not to move in beside another vehicle or into the blind spot of another vehicle.

Change lanes

Change lanes with a smooth, gradual movement into the new lane. Drive in the tire track that gives you the most space between vehicles in the lanes beside you.

Cancel signal

Turn off your signal as soon as you have changed lanes.

VI. ROADSIDE STOP

The approach
This driving task begins when the examiner tells you to stop and ends once you have come to a stop. Make sure you take these actions:

Traffic check
Before slowing down, check traffic in front and use your mirrors to check for traffic behind you. If there is a chance of traffic or pedestrians overtaking you on the right, check your right blind spot just before pulling over.

Signal
Turn on your signal before slowing down unless there are vehicles waiting to enter the road from sideroads or driveways between you and the point where you intend to stop. Wait until you have passed these entrances, so that drivers will not think you are turning before the stopping point.

Speed
Steadily reduce speed as you approach the stop. If your motorcycle is equipped with a clutch and gears, downshift into a lower gear as you slow down, but do not rely on downshifting only to slow down. Use both your front and rear brakes. This will also let other drivers know that you are slowing down. Come to a stop without weaving.

Position
Stop as far as possible off the travelled part of the road. Do not stop where you will block an entrance or other traffic.

The stop
This driving task includes the actions you take after stopping. Remember to do the following:

Signal
If your motorcycle or moped has four-way flashers, turn off your signal and turn on the four-way flashers.

Park
Depending on the parking surface, position your motorcycle or moped so it will be stable when the kick stand is down. Shift into neutral, or turn off the engine. Put the kick stand down.

Resume

This driving task begins when the examiner tells you to move back onto the road and ends when you have returned to normal traffic speed. Take the following actions:

Start

Holding the motorcycle or moped steady, put the kickstand up and start the engine, if necessary.

Signal

Turn off your four-way flashers and turn on your left signal.

Traffic check

Just before pulling away from the stop, check your mirrors and your left blind spot.

Speed

Return to normal traffic speed by accelerating smoothly to blend with the traffic around you. In light traffic, accelerate moderately.

In heavier traffic, you may have to accelerate more quickly. If your vehicle is equipped with gears, shift gears as you increase speed. Drive in the left tire track.

Cancel signal

Turn off your signal as soon as you are back on the road.

VII. CURVE

This driving task begins when the curve comes into sight and ends when you have gone completely around it. Follow these actions:

Speed

As you approach, try to determine the safe speed for the curve. To do this, look for clues such as a sign that shows the safe speed, the shape of the curve and the type of road you are driving on. Enter the curve at a safe speed. In a blind curve where you cannot see all the way around it, drive more slowly in case oncoming traffic wanders into your lane, or the curve is tighter than you expected. If your motorcycle has gears and you need to downshift, do so before entering the curve; do not shift gears in the curve. Not changing gears gives you more control over your motorcycle and reduces the risk of your wheels locking while downshifting. While in the curve, drive at a speed that balances the forces created by turning on the curve. Near the end of the curve, begin accelerating to return to normal speed.

Lane

As you enter the curve, look as far around it as possible. This helps you stay in a smooth line around the curve. If you look only at the road directly in front of you, you are likely to wander back and forth across the lane, constantly correcting your steering. On a curve with a short sight distance, drive in the tire track where you can see more of the road ahead. If the curve is to the left, use the right tire track. If the curve is to the right, keep as far left as possible while watching for oncoming traffic that might be cutting the curve short. You may also change tire tracks in order to drive through a more gradual curve than if you followed the full curve of the road.

VIII. BUSINESS SECTION

This driving task is done on straight sections of road where a number of businesses are located. Be sure to do the following actions:

Traffic check

In a business area, there are many places other than intersections where vehicles or pedestrians are likely to enter the road. These include entrances to businesses, institutions and construction sites, as well as pedestrian and railway crossings. At these and any other locations, look left and right to check for vehicles or pedestrians about to enter the road.

Mirror check

While driving along, check your mirrors every five to 10 seconds. Check your mirrors more often in heavy traffic or where vehicles are moving at different speeds.

Lane

Drive in the safest lane for through traffic. This is usually the curb lane. However, if the curb lane is blocked by traffic or there are many curbside hazards, the centre lane may be a safer choice. Drive in the best tire track for traffic conditions. Usually, this is the left tire track in the curb lane and the right tire track in the centre lane. Stay within the lane markings. Look ahead to where you will be in the next 12 to 15 seconds for dangerous situations or obstacles that you can avoid by changing lanes.

Speed

Avoid exceeding the speed limit or driving unreasonably slowly. Whenever possible, drive at a steady speed. Look ahead to where you will be in the next 12 to 15 seconds for dangerous situations or obstacles that you can avoid by changing your speed.

Space

Keep at least a two- to three-second distance behind the vehicle in front of you. Increase the distance if another vehicle follows too closely behind you. On a multi-lane road, try to keep a space on both sides of your motorcycle or moped, and try not to drive in the blind spots of other vehicles. In slow traffic, avoid driving behind large vehicles that block your view of traffic ahead of you.When you stop behind another vehicle, stay back at least a motorcycle length.

IX. RESIDENTIAL SECTION

This driving task is done on straight sections of residential or rural road. Remember these points:

Traffic check

On a residential road, watch out for entrances to schools, pedestrian crossings, driveways, sidewalks and any other locations where there might be traffic hazards. On rural roads, watch out for entrances to residences, farms, businesses and industrial sites. At all these locations, look left and right to check for vehicles or pedestrians about to enter the road.

Mirror check

While driving along, check your mirrors every five to 10 seconds. Check your mirrors more often in heavy traffic or where vehicles are moving at different speeds.

Lane

Generally, drive in the left tire track. If there are no lane markings, stay on the travelled part of the road. On a wide residential street, stay toward the centre of the road away from parked vehicles or pedestrians. Where you cannot see far ahead on the road because of a curve or a hill, drive in a tire track that will keep you from colliding with an oncoming vehicle that is over the centre line. Look ahead to where you will be in the next 12 to 15 seconds for dangerous situations or obstacles that you can avoid by changing lanes.

Speed

Avoid exceeding the speed limit or driving unreasonably slowly. Whenever possible, drive at a steady speed. Look ahead to where you will be in the next 12 to 15 seconds for dangerous situations or obstacles that you can avoid by changing your speed.

Space

Keep at least a two- to three-second distance behind the vehicle in front of you. Increase the distance if another vehicle follows too closely behind you. In slow traffic, avoid driving behind large vehicles that block your view of traffic ahead of you. When you stop behind another vehicle, stay behind at least one motorcycle length.

CONVERSION CHART

Imperial to Metric Converter

From	To	Multiply By
inches	centimetres	2.54
miles	kilometres	1.61
feet	metres	0.31
pounds	kilograms	0.46
miles per hour	kilometres per hour	1.61

Metric to Imperial Converter

From	To	Multiply By
centimetres	inches	0.39
kilometres	miles	0.62
metres	feet	3.28
kilograms	pounds	2.21
kilometres per hour	miles per hour	0.61

INDEX — THE OFFICIAL MTO MOTORCYCLE HANDBOOK

NOW THERE ARE MORE WAYS THAN EVER TO EXPRESS YOURSELF!

Personalize your licence plates — with two to eight characters, as well as a great choice of colour graphics. Then you'll really stand out from the crowd.

Turn the page to find out more.

WE'RE HELPING YOU BUILD CHARACTERS.

Now you've got extra choices when creating your personalized licence plate. We've introduced seven and eight characters. So you've got even more to work with — a minimum of two characters and right up to eight. Just think of the possibilities.

Every personalized plate is one of a kind. No one else can have the same plate as yours.

For more information and to order your personalized plates, call 1-800-AUTO-PL8 (1-800-288-6758).

**Or visit the ServiceOntario website: www.serviceontario.ca
Or drop by your local ServiceOntario centre.**

Gift certificates are available too.

Graphic licence plates are a hit! And now there are more than 40 choices available. Support your favourite Ontario sports team, community or arts organization, professional group or university. Or select a timeless icon like the loon or trillium.

For a totally unique look, add a colour graphic to a personalized plate with up to six characters.

So express yourself — with colour graphics and personalized licence plates.

For more information and to order your plates, call 1-800-AUTO-PL8 (1-800-288-6758).

**Or visit our website: www.mto.gov.on.ca
Or drop by your local ServiceOntario centre.**

*Gift certificates
are available too.*

ADD SOME COLOUR WHERE IT COUNTS.

OTHER MTO PUBLICATIONS FOR YOU

Copies of this handbook and others may be purchased from a:
- Retail store near you
- DriveTest Centre
- ServiceOntario Centre
- By calling (416) 326-5300 or 1-800-668-9938 (toll free)
- www.serviceontario.ca/publications

Prepayment required by credit card - VISA or Mastercard.
You may also pay with a certified cheque, bank draft or money order at DriveTest Centres.

Handbook and road map prices are subject to applicable H.S.T and shipping handling costs.

THE OFFICIAL DRIVER'S HANDBOOK

THE OFFICIAL MOTORCYCLE HANDBOOK

THE OFFICIAL TRUCK HANDBOOK

THE OFFICIAL BUS HANDBOOK

THE OFFICIAL AIR BRAKE HANDBOOK

THE OFFICIAL ONTARIO ROAD MAP